WHITBY
Travel Guide 2025

Unveiling the North Yorkshire Coast's Hidden Treasures, Iconic Attractions, and Heritage

Ronnie Sedlak

Copyright © 2024 Ronnie Sedlak

All rights reserved. This book cannot be duplicated, stored in a retrieval system, or transmitted in any way, including electronically, through recording, photocopying, scanning, or otherwise, without the copyright owner's prior written permission.

Table of Contents

Chapter 1 11

Welcome to Whitby 11

  An Introduction to Whitby 11

    Overview of Whitby's Location on the Yorkshire Coast 11

    Key Historical Milestones Shaping Whitby 12

    Why Whitby is a Must-Visit Destination in 2025 13

    Final Thoughts 14

  Geography and Natural Beauty 14

    Coastal Cliffs and Beaches: A Visual Treat 14

    River Esk's Influence on Whitby's Charm 15

    Seasonal Highlights and the Region's Flora and Fauna 16

    Why Geography and Natural Beauty Define Whitby 17

    Final Thoughts 17

  Essential Travel Information 17

    Best Times to Visit Whitby and Why 18

    Transportation Options: Trains, Buses, and Driving 19

    Overview of Accommodations: Hotels, B&Bs, and Vacation Rentals 20

    Why Essential Travel Information Matters 20

    Final Thoughts 21

Chapter 2 23

Historical Landmarks 23

  Whitby Abbey 23

    The Abbey's Role in Whitby's Religious and Cultural History 23

    Exploring the Ruins and the Stunning Coastal Views 24

    Bram Stoker's Connection to Whitby Abbey and Dracula 24

Why Whitby Abbey is a Must-Visit Landmark...25

Final Thoughts...25

199 Steps and Church of St. Mary..26

The Historical Significance of the 199 Steps..26

Highlights of the Church of St. Mary and Its Graveyard..26

Panoramic Views of Whitby from the Top...27

Why the 199 Steps and Church of St. Mary Are a Must-Visit.......................................28

Final Thoughts...28

Whitby Museum and Pannett Park...28

Local History Preserved at Whitby Museum...29

Maritime Artifacts and Fossil Displays..29

Strolling Through the Serene Pannett Park...30

Why Whitby Museum and Pannett Park Are Worth Visiting..31

Final Thoughts...31

Chapter 3   33
Whitby's Maritime Heritage   33

Captain Cook Memorial Museum..33

Captain James Cook's Early Years in Whitby..33

Exhibits Showcasing Cook's Voyages and Explorations...34

Insights into Whitby's Shipbuilding Legacy..34

Why the Captain Cook Memorial Museum is a Must-Visit..35

Final Thoughts...35

Whitby's Fishing Industry..36

The Evolution of Fishing in Whitby Over the Centuries...36

Traditional Practices and Modern Fishing Tours..36

Whitby's Famous Fish Market and Its Importance Today..........................37

Why Whitby's Fishing Industry Matters..38

Final Thoughts..38

The Whalebone Arch..39

The Story Behind This Iconic Landmark..39

Whitby's Whaling History in the 18th and 19th Centuries......................39

How the Arch Became a Symbol of Whitby...40

Why the Whalebone Arch Is a Must-Visit..41

Final Thoughts..41

Chapter 4   43
Beaches and Coastal Adventures   43

Whitby Beach and West Cliff..43

Family-Friendly Activities at Whitby Beach..43

Fossil Hunting and Rock Pooling at West Cliff.......................................44

Sunset Spots and Seaside Strolls..45

Why Whitby Beach and West Cliff Are Must-Visit Destinations...........46

Final Thoughts..46

Sandsend Beach..46

A Quieter Retreat for Relaxation and Surfing...46

Walking Trails Connecting Sandsend to Whitby....................................47

Dining Options Along the Sandsend Coast...48

Why Sandsend Beach Is a Must-Visit..49

Final Thoughts..49

Boat Trips and Coastal Cruises...49

Fishing Charters and Marine Tours...49

    The Famous Dracula Evening Cruises...50

    Wildlife Spotting from the Sea: Dolphins and Seabirds.............................51

    Why Boat Trips and Coastal Cruises Are Essential Experiences............... 52

    Final Thoughts... 52

Chapter 5   53

Gothic Whitby   53

    Whitby's Gothic Reputation.. 53

        How Dracula Popularized Whitby's Dark Charm.................................... 53

        Gothic Architecture and Its Presence in Whitby....................................... 54

        The Rise of Whitby's Gothic Subculture.. 54

        Why Whitby's Gothic Reputation Is Unmissable...................................... 55

        Final Thoughts.. 55

    Whitby Goth Weekend... 56

        Origins and Growth of This Unique Festival... 56

        Highlights: Parades, Fashion Shows, and Music Events.......................... 57

        How Visitors Can Participate or Spectate.. 58

        Why Whitby Goth Weekend Is a Must-Experience.................................. 59

        Final Thoughts.. 59

    Gothic Shopping and Art..59

        Specialty Shops Selling Gothic Fashion and Accessories.......................... 60

        Art Galleries Showcasing Gothic and Dracula-Inspired Works................ 60

        Souvenirs to Bring Home for Gothic Enthusiasts......................................61

        Why Gothic Shopping and Art Are Must-Experience Activities.............. 62

        Final Thoughts.. 62

Chapter 6   63

Food and Drink in Whitby 63

    Local Seafood and Fish and Chips... 63

        Whitby's Reputation for the Best Fish and Chips.. 63

        Renowned Seafood Restaurants and Takeaway Spots... 64

        Sustainability and Local Fishing Practices.. 65

        Why Local Seafood and Fish and Chips Are Must-Try Experiences........................... 65

        Final Thoughts.. 66

    Traditional Yorkshire Cuisine.. 66

        Must-Try Dishes: Yorkshire Pudding, Parkin, and More.. 66

        Pubs Offering Hearty Local Fare.. 67

        Farmers' Markets and Food Festivals.. 68

        Why Traditional Yorkshire Cuisine Is a Must-Try in Whitby...................................... 68

        Final Thoughts.. 69

    Whitby's Café and Pub Scene... 69

        Cozy Cafés with Homemade Desserts... 69

        Historic Pubs and Their Unique Stories... 70

        Local Ales and Gin Distilleries... 71

        Why Whitby's Café and Pub Scene Is Worth Exploring.. 72

        Final Thoughts.. 72

Chapter 7 73

Outdoor Adventures 73

    Walking and Hiking Trails... 73

        The Cleveland Way: Coastal Beauty on Foot... 73

        Trails Connecting Whitby to Robin Hood's Bay.. 74

        Easy Walks for Families with Children.. 75

Why Whitby's Walking and Hiking Trails Are a Must-Do...76

Final Thoughts...76

Cycling and Horse Riding...76

Cycle Paths Along the Coast and Through Moorlands..76

Horseback Riding Tours Near Whitby..77

Tips for Renting Gear and Guided Tours...78

Why Cycling and Horse Riding Are Unmissable in Whitby.......................................79

Final Thoughts...79

Watersports and Beach Activities...79

Kayaking and Paddleboarding Adventures...80

Surf Schools and Equipment Rentals...80

Swimming and Safety Tips for Families..81

Why Watersports and Beach Activities Are Unmissable in Whitby......................... 82

Final Thoughts...82

Chapter 8   **83**

Festivals and Events   **83**

Whitby Folk Week..83

Traditional Music and Dance Performances..83

Workshops and Interactive Events for Visitors..84

Family-Friendly Highlights of the Festival..85

Why Whitby Folk Week Is a Must-Attend Event...86

Final Thoughts...86

Regatta and Maritime Events..86

Whitby Regatta: A Mix of Races, Competitions, and Celebrations..........................87

Nautical Displays and Historical Reenactments..88

Evening Fireworks and Parades.. 88

Why Whitby Regatta and Maritime Events Are Unmissable............................... 89

Final Thoughts... 90

Christmas in Whitby... 90

Festive Markets and Decorations.. 90

Ice Skating and Seasonal Events.. 91

New Year's Eve Celebrations Along the Harbor.. 92

Why Christmas in Whitby Is Unmissable.. 93

Final Thoughts... 93

Chapter 9   95

Shopping and Local Crafts   95

Whitby Jet and Jewelry... 95

History of Whitby Jet Mining and Craftsmanship.. 95

Shops and Studios Specializing in Jet Jewelry.. 96

How to Identify Authentic Whitby Jet... 97

Why Whitby Jet Jewelry Is a Must-Buy Souvenir... 98

Final Thoughts... 98

Artisan Markets and Boutiques.. 98

Local Crafts and Handmade Souvenirs... 99

Farmers' Markets with Fresh Produce and Baked Goods................................ 99

Unique Gifts from Whitby's Independent Boutiques...................................... 100

Why Artisan Markets and Boutiques Are a Must-Visit.................................... 101

Final Thoughts... 102

Antiques and Vintage Finds... 102

Treasure Hunting in Whitby's Antique Shops.. 102

Vintage Fashion and Collectibles..103

Tips for Finding Hidden Gems... 104

Why Antiques and Vintage Finds Are a Must-Explore in Whitby.......................... 105

Final Thoughts...105

Chapter 10   107

Practical Tips for Visitors   107

Budget Travel Tips...107

Affordable Accommodations and Dining Options...107

Free Attractions and Activities... 108

Seasonal Discounts and Travel Passes...109

Why Budget Travel in Whitby Is Rewarding..110

Final Thoughts...110

Accessibility and Comfort... 110

Wheelchair-Friendly Routes and Attractions...111

Family-Friendly Amenities for Travelers with Kids...112

Tips for Stress-Free Navigation of Whitby..113

Why Accessibility and Comfort Matter in Whitby... 114

Final Thoughts...114

Packing and Preparation...114

What to Pack for Whitby's Coastal Climate..115

Essentials for Hiking, Festivals, and Boat Trips.. 116

Staying Connected with Wi-Fi and Mobile Services....................................... 117

Why Packing and Preparation Matter..118

Final Thoughts...118

Chapter 1
Welcome to Whitby

An Introduction to Whitby

Whitby, a picturesque seaside town on the Yorkshire coast, is a destination steeped in history, natural beauty, and cultural allure. Nestled between the dramatic cliffs of the North Sea and the serene countryside of North Yorkshire, Whitby has enchanted visitors for centuries. This section explores Whitby's geographic charm, its key historical milestones, and why it should be at the top of your travel list for 2025.

Overview of Whitby's Location on the Yorkshire Coast

Whitby is perched on the eastern coast of England, in North Yorkshire, at the mouth of the River Esk. This prime location is one of its defining features:

- **The North Sea Connection:** Whitby overlooks the North Sea, with its rugged coastline offering dramatic views, sandy beaches, and opportunities for maritime exploration.
- **A Gateway to the Moors:** The town serves as a key point of access to the sprawling **North York Moors National Park**, a haven for hikers and nature enthusiasts.
- **Proximity to Nearby Towns:** Situated approximately 47 miles from York and 20 miles from Scarborough, Whitby is easily accessible while still retaining its quaint, small-town charm.

The town's unique geography is further enriched by its iconic split:

- **East Cliff:** Home to the famous Whitby Abbey and St. Mary's Church, this side of the town is a historical treasure trove.
- **West Cliff:** Known for its sandy beach, colorful beach huts, and the iconic Whalebone Arch, West Cliff offers plenty of recreational activities.

Key Historical Milestones Shaping Whitby

Whitby's history is a tapestry woven with tales of monastic life, maritime triumphs, and literary inspiration:

- **The Founding of Whitby Abbey (657 AD):** Whitby's origins trace back to the establishment of Whitby Abbey by St. Hilda. The Abbey became a center of religious and cultural life in Anglo-Saxon England. It also hosted the Synod of Whitby in 664 AD, a significant event in shaping Christian practices in England.
- **Viking Influence:** Whitby's name derives from the Old Norse "Hvítabýr," meaning "white settlement." The Vikings left their mark on the town during their invasions in the 9th century.
- **The Whaling Industry (18th and 19th Century):** During the Georgian era, Whitby emerged as a thriving whaling hub, with its fleet venturing far into Arctic waters. The Whalebone Arch stands as a reminder of this period.

- **Captain Cook's Legacy:** Whitby is closely associated with Captain James Cook, one of the world's greatest explorers. Cook trained as a seaman in Whitby, and his legacy is preserved in the Captain Cook Memorial Museum.
- **Dracula and Bram Stoker (1897):** Whitby inspired Irish author Bram Stoker's *Dracula*. The haunting beauty of Whitby Abbey and its rugged coastline played a pivotal role in shaping the novel's gothic atmosphere.
- **The Rise of Tourism (Victorian Era):** With the advent of the railway in 1839, Whitby became a popular seaside retreat. Its promenade, beaches, and heritage attracted visitors from across England.

Why Whitby is a Must-Visit Destination in 2025

Whitby is a blend of the historic and the modern, offering experiences that cater to diverse interests:

- **Natural Beauty:** Whitby's coastline is part of the **Jurassic Coast**, a UNESCO World Heritage Site renowned for its fossil-rich cliffs. Visitors can explore geological wonders while enjoying breathtaking sea views.
- **Cultural Events:** Whitby is home to the **Whitby Goth Weekend**, a biannual festival celebrating gothic culture, and **Whitby Folk Week**, which showcases traditional music and dance. These events bring the town alive with color, music, and vibrancy.
- **Maritime Adventures:** From fishing charters to coastal cruises, Whitby offers plenty of opportunities to connect with its maritime roots. The harbor, with its charming boats and seafood eateries, is a hub of activity.
- **Gastronomy:** Whitby's seafood is legendary. No visit is complete without sampling freshly caught fish and chips or dining in its seafood restaurants overlooking the harbor.
- **Historic Landmarks:** Explore the ruins of **Whitby Abbey**, climb the iconic **199 Steps**, and visit the **Church of St. Mary**, all steeped in centuries of history.

- **Modern Amenities:** Whitby caters to travelers with a range of accommodations, from boutique hotels to cozy B&Bs, and its shops and galleries offer unique gifts and local art.

For 2025, Whitby is adding new events, guided tours, and eco-friendly initiatives, making it an even more appealing destination. Whether you're drawn by its literary connections, coastal beauty, or vibrant festivals, Whitby promises an unforgettable experience.

Final Thoughts

Whitby's location, history, and cultural significance make it a gem of the North Yorkshire coast. Whether you're marveling at the Abbey's ruins, strolling along sandy beaches, or immersing yourself in its gothic charm, Whitby offers something for everyone. As you plan your trip for 2025, prepare to uncover the secrets and treasures of this enchanting seaside town.

Geography and Natural Beauty

Whitby's geography and natural beauty are among its most captivating features, drawing travelers seeking coastal charm and tranquil scenery. From towering cliffs and picturesque beaches to the River Esk's tranquil influence and the diverse flora and fauna throughout the seasons, Whitby's landscape is a feast for the senses. This section delves into the visual allure of Whitby's coast, its riverside appeal, and the unique seasonal highlights that showcase its natural splendor.

Coastal Cliffs and Beaches: A Visual Treat

Whitby's coastline is characterized by dramatic cliffs, pristine beaches, and stunning views of the North Sea.

- **Towering Cliffs:** The cliffs along Whitby's coast, especially near East Cliff and Saltwick Bay, create a striking backdrop against the expansive blue of the sea.

These cliffs are rich in geological history, with layers of sediment revealing fossils and evidence of the Jurassic period.

- **Whitby Beach:** Stretching along the West Cliff, Whitby Beach is a sandy expanse perfect for families and leisure seekers. It's a hub for beach activities like building sandcastles, sunbathing, and paddling in the gentle waves.
- **Hidden Gems:** Nearby, **Sandsend Beach** offers a quieter alternative, with golden sands and a more tranquil atmosphere. **Robin Hood's Bay**, located a short drive from Whitby, is another scenic retreat, known for its steep streets leading to a picturesque shoreline.
- **Sunsets Over the North Sea:** Whitby's coastal geography makes it an ideal spot to witness breathtaking sunsets, with hues of orange, pink, and purple reflecting off the water.

The unique combination of cliffs, beaches, and panoramic views makes Whitby's coast a visual and recreational delight, offering something for every traveler.

River Esk's Influence on Whitby's Charm

The **River Esk** is central to Whitby's identity, dividing the town into two distinct halves connected by the iconic **Swing Bridge**. Its gentle flow shapes the town's scenery and activities:

- **Historic Harbor:** The River Esk opens into Whitby's harbor, a bustling area lined with fishing boats, yachts, and leisure vessels. The harbor's charm is enhanced by its cobbled streets, historic buildings, and seafood eateries.
- **Waterside Walks:** Strolling along the riverbanks offers picturesque views of Whitby's landmarks, such as the Abbey on the East Cliff and the colorful beach huts on the West Cliff.
- **Wildlife Spotting:** The river is home to diverse wildlife, including otters, kingfishers, and swans. Visitors often enjoy observing these creatures from quiet riverbank vantage points.
- **Cultural Influence:** The River Esk also plays a vital role in Whitby's maritime traditions, from its history as a whaling port to its modern fishing industry.

The river's calm presence contrasts beautifully with the rugged cliffs and energetic coastline, adding depth and tranquility to Whitby's landscape.

Seasonal Highlights and the Region's Flora and Fauna

Whitby's natural beauty evolves with the seasons, offering distinct highlights year-round:

- **Spring:**
    - Whitby's countryside comes alive with blooms of daffodils, bluebells, and wildflowers.
    - Migratory birds return to the area, filling the air with their songs. Coastal cliffs and moorlands become lush with new growth, creating stunning vistas.
- **Summer:**
    - Whitby's beaches and coastal trails are at their peak, attracting sunseekers and adventurers alike.
    - Wildlife enthusiasts can spot puffins and other seabirds along the cliffs, while dolphins occasionally grace the waters near the shore.
    - The warm weather also highlights the beauty of nearby **North York Moors**, with purple heather carpeting the hillsides.
- **Autumn:**
    - The landscape transforms into a tapestry of golden hues, with trees and moorlands displaying vibrant autumn foliage.
    - Autumn is a prime time for spotting deer in the surrounding woodlands and coastal hills.
    - Harvest festivals and seasonal markets in Whitby celebrate the bounty of the season.
- **Winter:**
    - Though quieter, Whitby's winter landscape offers a serene beauty, with snow-dusted cliffs and frosty mornings.
    - Seals can sometimes be spotted basking on the shores, and the harbor exudes a festive charm during the holiday season.

- Winter walks along the River Esk or the coastal trails are perfect for those seeking peace and solitude.

From its floral displays in spring to its wildlife encounters in summer and winter, Whitby's seasonal changes make it a year-round destination for nature lovers.

Why Geography and Natural Beauty Define Whitby

Whitby's unique blend of coastal cliffs, serene riverbanks, and seasonal highlights sets it apart as a destination that appeals to every traveler:

- **For Scenic Seekers:** The cliffs and beaches provide endless opportunities for photography, relaxation, and exploration.
- **For Nature Enthusiasts:** The River Esk and surrounding moorlands offer a tranquil escape filled with wildlife and natural wonders.
- **For Year-Round Travelers:** Each season brings its charm, ensuring there's always something new to discover in Whitby's ever-changing landscape.

Final Thoughts

Whitby's geography and natural beauty are integral to its allure, offering visitors a harmonious blend of rugged coastline, serene riverscapes, and diverse seasonal experiences. Whether you're watching a fiery sunset over the cliffs, exploring the vibrant riverbanks, or marveling at the changing flora and fauna, Whitby's natural landscape promises to captivate your heart and imagination.

Essential Travel Information

Whitby is a year-round destination with unique charms that vary by season, making it vital for visitors to plan their trip with key information in mind. From deciding on the best times to visit, to navigating the town with convenient transportation options, and choosing the perfect accommodation, this section provides practical tips to ensure a seamless travel experience.

Best Times to Visit Whitby and Why

Whitby offers something special in every season, but the timing of your visit can significantly influence your experience:

- **Spring (March to May):**
    - ➢ **Why Visit?** Spring is ideal for those who enjoy fewer crowds and mild weather. Wildflowers bloom across the surrounding North York Moors, and wildlife like migratory birds and seals become more active.
    - ➢ **Events:** The annual Whitby Goth Weekend typically occurs in April, drawing visitors from around the world for its vibrant mix of gothic culture and music.
- **Summer (June to August):**
    - ➢ **Why Visit?** Summer is peak season, with long daylight hours perfect for exploring beaches, hiking trails, and outdoor attractions. Families flock to Whitby's sandy shores for sunbathing and rock pooling.
    - ➢ **Events:** Whitby Folk Week in August offers a week-long celebration of traditional music and dance, adding a festive atmosphere to the town.
- **Autumn (September to November):**
    - ➢ **Why Visit?** The autumn months bring cooler weather, fewer tourists, and stunning fall foliage in the nearby countryside. This is a fantastic time for photographers and nature enthusiasts.
    - ➢ **Events:** September's Heritage Open Days allow visitors to explore historical sites, including Whitby Abbey, often with free entry and guided tours.
- **Winter (December to February):**
    - ➢ **Why Visit?** Winter in Whitby is peaceful, with its cobbled streets and harbor adorned with festive lights. It's a magical time to explore without crowds.
    - ➢ **Events:** Christmas markets and New Year's celebrations add seasonal cheer, while the winter seas provide dramatic coastal views.

Each season highlights a different aspect of Whitby's charm, ensuring there's no wrong time to visit.

Transportation Options: Trains, Buses, and Driving

Whitby is well-connected, making it accessible for travelers from across the UK.

- **Trains:**
    - The nearest major rail station is in Middlesbrough, with connecting services to Whitby operated by **Northern Rail**. The scenic **Esk Valley Line** offers picturesque views of the North York Moors, making the journey an experience in itself.
    - Travel Tip: Booking advance tickets can save money, especially during peak travel periods.
- **Buses:**
    - Regional bus services, such as those operated by **Arriva North East**, connect Whitby to nearby towns like Scarborough and York. Long-distance coach services are also available for budget-conscious travelers.
    - Travel Tip: The local **Coastal Explorer Bus Pass** provides unlimited travel across key destinations along the Yorkshire coast.
- **Driving:**
    - For travelers with cars, Whitby is accessible via the A171 road, which links the town to Middlesbrough and Scarborough. Parking can be challenging during peak seasons, so arrive early to secure a spot.
    - Travel Tip: Park-and-ride facilities on the outskirts of Whitby help reduce congestion in the town center.
- **Additional Options:**
    - Cyclists can enjoy dedicated routes like the **Cinder Track**, a scenic trail connecting Whitby to Scarborough.
    - Taxis are available for short-distance travel or late-night returns from pubs and events.

Overview of Accommodations: Hotels, B&Bs, and Vacation Rentals

Whitby offers a wide range of accommodations catering to different budgets and preferences:

- **Hotels:**
    - **Luxury Options:** Upscale hotels like **Raithwaite Sandsend** offer elegant rooms, spa facilities, and proximity to the beach.
    - **Mid-Range:** Options like **The Angel Hotel**, located near the harbor, provide modern amenities and excellent views at reasonable prices.
- **Bed and Breakfasts (B&Bs):**
    - Whitby is renowned for its cozy B&Bs, many of which are housed in charming historic buildings. Favorites include **The White House Inn** and **Abbotsleigh of Whitby**, both praised for their warm hospitality and hearty breakfasts.
    - B&Bs are a great choice for travelers seeking a more personal touch.
- **Vacation Rentals:**
    - Cottages and holiday homes, such as those offered by **Sykes Cottages** and **Airbnb**, are popular among families and groups. Many rentals feature fully equipped kitchens and private gardens, ideal for longer stays.
    - Coastal properties with sea views are highly sought after, especially near West Cliff or Sandsend.
- **Budget-Friendly Options:**
    - Hostels like **YHA Whitby**, located near Whitby Abbey, offer affordable lodging with communal facilities.
    - Campsites and caravan parks, such as those near Robin Hood's Bay, are ideal for outdoor enthusiasts.

Travelers should book accommodations well in advance, particularly during peak seasons and major events, as Whitby's popularity can lead to limited availability.

Why Essential Travel Information Matters

Understanding the best times to visit, transportation options, and accommodation choices ensures your Whitby trip is both enjoyable and stress-free:

- **For Seasonal Planners:** Timing your visit to align with your interests, whether it's festivals or peaceful winter strolls, enhances your experience.
- **For Navigational Ease:** Knowing how to get around Whitby helps you make the most of your time.
- **For Comfortable Stays:** Choosing the right accommodation ensures a restful and memorable trip.

Final Thoughts

Planning your trip to Whitby becomes effortless with an understanding of seasonal highlights, transportation routes, and accommodations. Whether you're arriving by train, exploring by bus, or settling into a quaint seaside B&B, Whitby's accessibility and charm guarantee an unforgettable adventure. Prepare to experience the town's magic in every season and make the most of its welcoming hospitality.

Chapter 2
Historical Landmarks

Whitby Abbey

Whitby Abbey is more than just a historic site; it is the beating heart of Whitby's religious, cultural, and literary heritage. Towering over the coastal cliffs, the Abbey's ruins have stood the test of time, captivating visitors with their gothic beauty and rich history. This section explores the Abbey's profound influence on the town, the experience of exploring its majestic ruins, and its pivotal role in Bram Stoker's *Dracula*.

The Abbey's Role in Whitby's Religious and Cultural History

Whitby Abbey has been a cornerstone of religious and cultural life in North Yorkshire for centuries.

- **Foundation and Early Significance:** The Abbey was founded in 657 AD by **King Oswiu of Northumbria** and presided over by **St. Hilda**, a revered figure in Christian history. It became an important religious center during Anglo-Saxon England, playing a critical role in shaping early Christian practices.
    - The **Synod of Whitby** in 664 AD, held at the Abbey, resolved disputes between Celtic and Roman Christian traditions, leading to the adoption of the Roman system for calculating Easter. This event was pivotal in unifying Christian practices across England.
- **Medieval Prosperity:** Rebuilt in the 11th century after Viking destruction, the Abbey flourished as a Benedictine monastery. It became a hub for learning, art, and agriculture, contributing significantly to the region's economic and cultural growth.
- **Dissolution and Decline:** During **Henry VIII's Dissolution of the Monasteries** in the 16th century, Whitby Abbey was closed, and its wealth confiscated. The Abbey's decline began, leaving the hauntingly beautiful ruins that stand today as a testament to its former glory.

Whitby Abbey's enduring presence continues to inspire awe, connecting modern visitors with the town's deep-rooted history.

Exploring the Ruins and the Stunning Coastal Views

Visiting Whitby Abbey is an immersive experience that combines history with breathtaking natural beauty.

- **Majestic Ruins:** The Abbey's soaring arches and intricate stonework are remarkable examples of **Gothic architecture**. As visitors walk through the site, they can marvel at the craftsmanship that has withstood centuries of weather and war.
  - ➢ Informational plaques and audio guides detail the Abbey's history, bringing the ruins to life with stories of monks, kings, and invasions.
- **Coastal Views:** Perched atop the **East Cliff**, the Abbey offers panoramic views of the North Sea, Whitby Harbor, and the surrounding countryside. These vistas are particularly stunning during sunrise or sunset, when the light bathes the ruins in a golden glow.
  - ➢ Visitors can also enjoy a view of the **199 Steps**, a historic staircase leading from the harbor to the Abbey, providing a sense of connection between the town and its iconic landmark.
- **Events and Activities:** Whitby Abbey often hosts special events, including **reenactments**, **historical tours**, and **seasonal festivals**. These activities enhance the visitor experience, offering a deeper understanding of life at the Abbey throughout its history.

Bram Stoker's Connection to Whitby Abbey and Dracula

Whitby Abbey is forever linked to the literary world through **Bram Stoker**, the Irish author of the classic gothic novel *Dracula*.

- **Stoker's Visit to Whitby:** Stoker visited Whitby in 1890, staying at the **Royal Crescent**. Captivated by the eerie beauty of the Abbey ruins and the dramatic coastal setting, he found inspiration for his novel's chilling atmosphere.

- ➢ The Abbey, with its towering arches and weathered stone, served as a visual template for **Castle Dracula**, the vampire's Transylvanian lair.
- **Dracula's Arrival in Whitby:** In the novel, Stoker depicts **Count Dracula's arrival** in England through the wreck of the ship **Demeter**, which runs aground near Whitby. The image of Dracula's dark figure leaping from the wreck and transforming into a dog is a powerful moment in the story, forever tying the Abbey to gothic lore.
- **Modern-Day Legacy:** Whitby embraces its connection to *Dracula* with themed events, including the **Whitby Goth Weekend**, and souvenirs that pay homage to Stoker's work. The Abbey itself is a focal point for gothic enthusiasts, drawing visitors eager to explore the birthplace of literary horror.

Why Whitby Abbey is a Must-Visit Landmark

Whitby Abbey is more than a historical site—it is a symbol of Whitby's identity:

- **For History Buffs:** The Abbey offers a window into Anglo-Saxon and medieval life, as well as England's religious evolution.
- **For Photographers:** The interplay of dramatic ruins and coastal views provides endless opportunities for stunning photography.
- **For Literature Lovers:** Fans of *Dracula* can immerse themselves in the gothic ambiance that inspired one of the world's most famous novels.

Final Thoughts

Whitby Abbey is a place where history, culture, and literature converge. Its towering ruins tell the story of a bygone era, while its breathtaking views and connection to Bram Stoker's *Dracula* continue to inspire visitors. Whether you're exploring its rich history, marveling at the architectural beauty, or retracing the steps of literary legend, Whitby Abbey offers an unforgettable experience. A visit to this iconic landmark is a journey through time, offering a deeper appreciation for the legacy of Whitby and its place in history.

199 Steps and Church of St. Mary

The **199 Steps** and the **Church of St. Mary** are iconic landmarks that embody Whitby's historical charm and spiritual heritage. Climbing these steps is not just a journey through Whitby's rich past but also an opportunity to witness breathtaking views of the town and its dramatic coastline. This section explores the historical significance of the steps, the highlights of the Church of St. Mary and its ancient graveyard, and the panoramic vistas awaiting visitors at the top.

The Historical Significance of the 199 Steps

The **199 Steps** have been a vital part of Whitby's landscape for centuries, serving as both a functional and symbolic connection between the harbor and the East Cliff.

- **Origins and Purpose:** The steps were originally constructed to provide easier access to **Whitby Abbey** and the Church of St. Mary. Pilgrims would ascend them as part of their journey to visit the Abbey, viewing the climb as a spiritual act of devotion.
  - Early records suggest that the steps were made of wood, later replaced by stone to endure the test of time.
- **Cultural Legacy:** The 199 Steps are deeply rooted in Whitby's identity. They have been referenced in art, literature, and local folklore, symbolizing the resilience and history of the town.
  - Local legends include tales of how fishermen would ascend the steps to seek blessings for their voyages.
- **Modern-Day Appeal:** Today, the 199 Steps attract thousands of visitors annually, offering a blend of exercise, history, and stunning rewards at the summit. Along the way, resting spots allow climbers to pause, reflect, and take in the views of the harbor below.

Highlights of the Church of St. Mary and Its Graveyard

At the top of the 199 Steps lies the **Church of St. Mary**, a site of immense historical and architectural significance.

- **Architectural Features:** The Church of St. Mary dates back to the 12th century, with elements of **Norman and Gothic design**. Its simple yet striking structure includes a square tower and medieval interiors.
  - Inside, visitors can admire intricately carved pews, box pews unique to the era, and maritime-themed memorials reflecting Whitby's seafaring heritage.
- **The Graveyard:** The churchyard is one of the most atmospheric spots in Whitby. It is famously depicted in **Bram Stoker's *Dracula***, where it serves as a haunting setting for key scenes in the novel.
  - The gravestones, weathered by time and the sea breeze, tell stories of Whitby's past, from shipwrecked sailors to notable locals.
  - Many visitors are captivated by the graveyard's eerie beauty, enhanced by its cliffside perch overlooking the town.
- **Spiritual Importance:** The Church of St. Mary continues to serve as a place of worship, hosting services and community events. Its historical and spiritual significance makes it a cornerstone of Whitby's cultural identity.

Panoramic Views of Whitby from the Top

The ascent up the 199 Steps is richly rewarded with **breathtaking views** that showcase the beauty and character of Whitby.

- **Harbor and Townscape:** From the summit, visitors can gaze down upon Whitby's bustling harbor, with its colorful fishing boats and cobbled streets. The view captures the essence of the town's maritime heritage and lively charm.
  - The rooftops of Whitby's historic buildings spread out below, creating a picturesque scene that feels like stepping back in time.
- **Coastal Splendor:** The cliffs of the Yorkshire coast and the expanse of the North Sea stretch out on the horizon. On clear days, the view is particularly stunning, with the sparkling waters reflecting the sky's hues.
  - The vantage point also offers a closer look at the dramatic ruins of **Whitby Abbey**, framed against the coastal backdrop.

- **Sunrise and Sunset Views:** For an unforgettable experience, visitors are encouraged to climb the steps during sunrise or sunset. The soft light transforms the landscape, casting a golden glow over the town and the sea.

Why the 199 Steps and Church of St. Mary Are a Must-Visit

The **199 Steps** and **Church of St. Mary** represent the heart of Whitby's history, spirituality, and scenic allure:

- **For History Enthusiasts:** The steps and church are living testaments to Whitby's religious and cultural evolution.
- **For Literature Fans:** The connection to *Dracula* and the graveyard's atmospheric setting make this spot a literary pilgrimage.
- **For Scenic Seekers:** The panoramic views from the top are among the most iconic and rewarding in Whitby.

Final Thoughts

Climbing the **199 Steps** and visiting the **Church of St. Mary** is more than a physical journey—it's a step into Whitby's rich past and breathtaking present. Whether you're drawn by history, inspired by literature, or simply seeking awe-inspiring views, this landmark is an essential part of any visit to Whitby. Prepare to be enchanted by the stories, scenery, and spirit of this remarkable place.

Whitby Museum and Pannett Park

Whitby Museum and Pannett Park combine history, culture, and natural beauty, making them a must-visit destination for anyone exploring Whitby. The museum houses a treasure trove of local artifacts, from maritime relics to fossils, while the park provides a peaceful escape into nature. Together, they offer a glimpse into Whitby's heritage and a chance to unwind amidst lush greenery.

Local History Preserved at Whitby Museum

Located in the heart of Pannett Park, **Whitby Museum** is a testament to the town's rich history and community pride.

- **Foundation and Community Roots:** Established in 1823 by the Whitby Literary and Philosophical Society, the museum has been preserving and showcasing Whitby's heritage for over two centuries. Its collections, built through donations and careful curation, reflect the unique character of the town and its people.
- **Exhibits of Local Significance:**
    - **Jet Jewelry and Craftsmanship:** Whitby is famous for its jet, a fossilized wood used to create stunning jewelry during the Victorian era. The museum's exhibits highlight the history of jet mining and the craftsmanship that made it a sought-after material.
    - **Historical Artifacts:** From tools used by early settlers to items reflecting the town's industrial past, the museum provides a comprehensive look at Whitby's development over the years.
- **Literary Connections:** The museum's collections include items linked to **Bram Stoker**, offering additional insights into the author's time in Whitby and the inspiration behind *Dracula*.

Maritime Artifacts and Fossil Displays

Whitby's maritime legacy and its position along the Jurassic Coast are celebrated through fascinating exhibits in the museum.

- **Maritime Heritage:**
    - **Ship Models and Nautical Instruments:** The museum's maritime collection features intricately detailed ship models, navigational tools, and personal items belonging to sailors, showcasing Whitby's seafaring history.

- ➢ **Captain Cook Connection:** Whitby's association with Captain James Cook is prominently displayed, including models of the ships he sailed on, such as the famous **HMS Endeavour.**
- Fossil and Geology Exhibits:
  - ➢ **Jurassic Coast Fossils:** As part of the world-famous Jurassic Coast, Whitby is a hotspot for fossil discoveries. The museum houses an extensive collection of ammonites, ichthyosaurs, and other prehistoric remains found along the Yorkshire coastline.
  - ➢ **Interactive Displays:** Visitors can learn about the region's geological history and the techniques used to uncover these ancient treasures.

These exhibits make Whitby Museum a fascinating destination for both history enthusiasts and geology buffs, offering a window into the town's past and its connection to the natural world.

Strolling Through the Serene Pannett Park

Surrounding the museum is **Pannett Park**, a beautifully landscaped green space that offers a tranquil retreat from Whitby's bustling streets.

- **History of the Park:**
  - ➢ Donated by Robert Pannett in the early 20th century, the park was designed to provide a space for relaxation and community events. Today, it remains a cherished part of Whitby's cultural landscape.
- **Gardens and Scenic Walkways:**
  - ➢ The park features manicured gardens with seasonal flowers, mature trees, and scenic walkways. It's a perfect spot for leisurely strolls, picnics, or simply enjoying the fresh sea air.
  - ➢ Highlights include the **Rose Garden** and **Lily Pond**, which provide picturesque backdrops for photography.

- **Play Area and Family-Friendly Features:**
    - A dedicated children's play area ensures that families with young ones can enjoy the park as much as adults. Educational signage and wildlife spotting opportunities make it a great place for kids to learn about nature.
- **Art and Community Events:**
    - Pannett Park hosts regular art installations and community events, enhancing its appeal as a cultural hub. Seasonal activities, such as guided nature walks and outdoor theater performances, bring the park to life.

Why Whitby Museum and Pannett Park Are Worth Visiting

Whitby Museum and Pannett Park provide an enriching and relaxing experience that showcases the essence of Whitby:

- **For History Buffs:** The museum's extensive collections cover everything from maritime history to geology, offering deep insights into the town's heritage.
- **For Nature Lovers:** The park's lush greenery and peaceful atmosphere provide a perfect counterbalance to the town's busy harbor.
- **For Families:** Interactive exhibits in the museum and kid-friendly features in the park make it a great day out for visitors of all ages.

Final Thoughts

Whitby Museum and Pannett Park are treasures that capture the spirit of Whitby, combining education, culture, and natural beauty. Whether you're exploring the museum's captivating exhibits, marveling at fossils and maritime relics, or enjoying a relaxing stroll through the park, this duo promises an experience that is both enlightening and rejuvenating. A visit here is essential to truly appreciate the depth and diversity of Whitby's charm.

Chapter 3
Whitby's Maritime Heritage

Captain Cook Memorial Museum

The **Captain Cook Memorial Museum** in Whitby offers a fascinating look at the life and legacy of one of history's greatest explorers, Captain James Cook. Housed in the very building where Cook lived during his early years, the museum is a treasure trove of artifacts, exhibits, and stories that highlight his profound connection to Whitby and his pivotal role in global exploration. This section explores Cook's formative years in Whitby, the museum's exhibits, and insights into Whitby's shipbuilding legacy that supported his remarkable journeys.

Captain James Cook's Early Years in Whitby

Captain James Cook, renowned for his exploratory voyages across the Pacific, spent critical formative years in Whitby that laid the foundation for his illustrious career.

- **Apprenticeship in Whitby:** In 1746, at the age of 17, Cook moved to Whitby to begin an apprenticeship under the **Walker family**, prominent Quaker shipowners and coal merchants. This apprenticeship was a transformative period during which Cook gained hands-on experience in navigation, seamanship, and ship maintenance. He worked aboard Whitby-built colliers—sturdy coal transport ships that would later serve as models for his exploration vessels.
- **Living at Grape Lane:** The building that now houses the museum was Cook's home during his apprenticeship. Situated on **Grape Lane**, this Georgian townhouse provided Cook with a base as he trained to master the skills necessary for a seafaring career. The house itself has been beautifully preserved, allowing visitors to step back in time and see where Cook's journey began.
- **Whitby's Influence:** Whitby's bustling harbor, dynamic shipbuilding industry, and access to the North Sea provided Cook with the environment he needed to develop into a skilled navigator and mariner. These years not only shaped his professional abilities but also ignited his passion for exploration.

Exhibits Showcasing Cook's Voyages and Explorations

The Captain Cook Memorial Museum offers a detailed exploration of Cook's three groundbreaking voyages, which transformed the understanding of the world during the 18th century.

- **Charting the Pacific:** Exhibits feature maps, journals, and sketches created during Cook's expeditions. These include:
    - His first voyage aboard the **HMS Endeavour**, which mapped the east coast of Australia and observed the transit of Venus.
    - His second voyage aboard the **Resolution**, during which he ventured further south than any explorer had before, coming close to Antarctica.
    - His third and final voyage, which sought the elusive Northwest Passage and led to his untimely death in Hawaii.
- **Artifacts from the Voyages:** The museum houses an array of fascinating objects brought back from Cook's travels, including:
    - **Polynesian tools and art** that highlight the cultural exchanges between Cook's crew and the indigenous peoples of the Pacific.
    - **Natural history specimens,** including botanical illustrations by Joseph Banks, who accompanied Cook on his first voyage.
    - **Navigational tools** used by Cook, showcasing the innovation and skill required for long-distance sea voyages in the 18th century.
- **Interactive Learning:** For visitors, the museum offers hands-on displays, videos, and guided tours to make Cook's achievements accessible and engaging. These exhibits not only celebrate his accomplishments but also provide a nuanced view of the impact of exploration on the world's indigenous cultures.

Insights into Whitby's Shipbuilding Legacy

Whitby's shipbuilding industry played a vital role in supporting Captain Cook's voyages and shaping the town's maritime heritage.

- **Sturdy Colliers:** Cook's exploration vessels, such as the HMS Endeavour, were modeled on Whitby colliers—durable, flat-bottomed ships designed for transporting coal. These ships were known for their resilience and ability to navigate treacherous waters, making them ideal for long exploratory missions.
- **Whitby's Shipyards:** During Cook's time, Whitby was a thriving hub for shipbuilding. The town's shipyards produced vessels that were celebrated for their craftsmanship and practicality. The Walker family, Cook's employers, were among the leading figures in this industry, contributing significantly to Whitby's maritime prominence.
- **Connection to Global Exploration:** The ships built in Whitby not only supported Cook's expeditions but also played a role in the broader expansion of British trade and exploration. This legacy is evident in the town's harbor, where visitors can still see traditional shipbuilding techniques on display during festivals and events.

Why the Captain Cook Memorial Museum is a Must-Visit

The Captain Cook Memorial Museum is a vital destination for anyone interested in Whitby's maritime heritage and the story of one of the world's greatest explorers.

- **For History Enthusiasts:** The museum provides a comprehensive look at Cook's life, from his humble beginnings to his transformative voyages.
- **For Aspiring Mariners:** The exhibits offer inspiration through Cook's journey of learning and perseverance.
- **For Families:** Interactive displays and guided tours make it an engaging experience for visitors of all ages.

Final Thoughts

The **Captain Cook Memorial Museum** is not just a celebration of one man's achievements; it's a tribute to Whitby's enduring maritime legacy and its role in shaping global history. Through exhibits on Cook's life, voyages, and the town's shipbuilding heritage, visitors gain a deeper appreciation for Whitby's place on the world map.

Whether you're marveling at artifacts from the Pacific or standing in the very house where Cook's journey began, this museum offers a truly enriching experience that connects the past to the present.

Whitby's Fishing Industry

Whitby's fishing industry has been a cornerstone of the town's economy and culture for centuries. From its humble beginnings as a small fishing village to its status as a bustling harbor town, Whitby has been shaped by the rhythm of the sea. This section explores the evolution of Whitby's fishing industry, traditional practices and modern fishing tours, and the role of Whitby's fish market in preserving this enduring heritage.

The Evolution of Fishing in Whitby Over the Centuries

Fishing has been central to Whitby's identity since its earliest days.

- **Medieval Foundations:** During the medieval period, Whitby was a modest fishing village that relied heavily on the bounty of the North Sea. The River Esk provided safe access to the ocean, and fishing became a way of life for the town's residents.
- **The Whaling Era:** In the 18th and early 19th centuries, Whitby expanded its maritime activities to include whaling. The town's fleet ventured into Arctic waters, bringing back whale oil and blubber, which were in high demand during the Industrial Revolution. This era saw Whitby's economy flourish, with the fishing industry growing in parallel to support the needs of local and regional markets.
- **Transition to Modern Fishing:** As whaling declined, Whitby returned its focus to traditional fishing practices. The introduction of steam-powered trawlers in the late 19th century revolutionized the industry, allowing fishermen to venture further out to sea and bring back larger catches. The 20th century brought further advancements in fishing gear and techniques, ensuring Whitby's place as a leading fishing port along the Yorkshire coast.

Traditional Practices and Modern Fishing Tours

Whitby's fishing heritage is preserved through traditional practices and has adapted to cater to modern tourism, offering visitors a glimpse into this enduring way of life.

- **Traditional Practices:**
    - **Cobles and Nets:** Historically, Whitby fishermen used distinctive flat-bottomed boats known as **cobles**, which were well-suited for the region's shallow coastal waters. Fishing involved longlines, nets, and traps, with catches including cod, herring, and mackerel.
    - **Seasonal Patterns:** Fishing was heavily influenced by the seasons, with different species caught at various times of the year. The herring season, in particular, was a major event, bringing the community together.
- **Modern Fishing Tours:**
    - **Chartered Fishing Trips:** Today, Whitby's fishing industry caters to locals and tourists alike through chartered fishing tours. Visitors can join professional crews for half-day or full-day excursions, experiencing the thrill of catching species like cod, haddock, and skate.
    - **Hands-On Experiences:** These tours often include tutorials on traditional fishing techniques, allowing participants to learn how to cast lines, set traps, and clean their catches.
    - **Family-Friendly Activities:** Many fishing tours are designed to be family-friendly, offering opportunities for children to learn about marine life and sustainability while enjoying the open sea.

Fishing tours not only provide an authentic maritime experience but also support the local economy by celebrating Whitby's fishing traditions.

Whitby's Famous Fish Market and Its Importance Today

The **Whitby Fish Market** remains a vibrant hub of activity, connecting the town's fishing industry to residents, visitors, and businesses.

- **Fresh Catch Daily:** The fish market is known for its fresh, high-quality seafood, brought in daily by Whitby's fleet. Local fishermen supply the market with a variety of species, including haddock, cod, plaice, and lobster.
- **Community Connection:** The market plays a crucial role in Whitby's culinary identity, supplying fish to local restaurants, fish and chip shops, and home cooks. It's also a gathering place for residents, who rely on its offerings to maintain a tradition of fresh, locally sourced seafood.
- **Sustainability Efforts:** Whitby's fish market has embraced sustainable fishing practices to protect marine ecosystems and ensure the industry's future. Efforts include supporting quotas and responsible fishing methods, ensuring that Whitby's waters remain productive for generations to come.
- **Visitor Experience:** Visitors to the fish market can witness the bustling energy of a traditional seafood marketplace. Early mornings are particularly exciting, as the day's catch is auctioned off to local buyers. Some stalls also offer direct sales, allowing tourists to purchase seafood to enjoy during their stay.

Why Whitby's Fishing Industry Matters

Whitby's fishing industry is more than an economic activity; it's a living testament to the town's resilience and adaptability.

- **For History Buffs:** The evolution of fishing in Whitby offers insights into how the town has navigated changing times while staying rooted in its maritime traditions.
- **For Foodies:** The fish market and local seafood offerings make Whitby a paradise for lovers of fresh, flavorful cuisine.
- **For Visitors:** Modern fishing tours provide an unforgettable way to connect with Whitby's maritime heritage, offering hands-on experiences that blend education with adventure.

Final Thoughts

Whitby's fishing industry has weathered centuries of change, evolving from medieval cobles and whaling fleets to modern trawlers and sustainable practices. Through its fish market, traditional techniques, and fishing tours, this legacy remains a vital part of the town's identity. A visit to Whitby is incomplete without exploring its fishing heritage, whether by savoring freshly caught seafood, embarking on a fishing trip, or immersing yourself in the vibrant atmosphere of the fish market. This enduring connection to the sea ensures Whitby's place as a beacon of maritime history and culture.

The Whalebone Arch

The **Whalebone Arch** is one of Whitby's most iconic landmarks, symbolizing the town's maritime heritage and its historical connection to the whaling industry. Located on the West Cliff, the arch frames stunning views of Whitby Abbey and the North Sea, drawing visitors from around the world. This section delves into the story behind this unique structure, Whitby's whaling history in the 18th and 19th centuries, and how the arch has become a lasting symbol of Whitby.

The Story Behind This Iconic Landmark

The Whalebone Arch is a striking feature that has stood as a gateway to Whitby's seafaring past.

- **Origins of the Arch:** The current arch, installed in **2003**, is made from the jawbones of a bowhead whale, donated by Alaska's Inuit community as a tribute to Whitby's whaling legacy. It replaced an earlier version erected in **1963**, which itself had replaced the original arch dating back to the 19th century.
    - Each iteration of the arch has reinforced Whitby's historical connection to the whaling industry, serving as a memorial to the town's maritime past.
- **Significance of the Location:** Positioned on **West Cliff**, the Whalebone Arch overlooks the harbor, with views of **Whitby Abbey** and the coastline. This location emphasizes the town's intertwined relationship with the sea and its industries.

- **Symbolism of the Arch:** The structure represents both the economic importance of whaling to Whitby and a reminder of the cost to nature. In modern times, it has also come to symbolize the town's commitment to preserving its history while acknowledging environmental responsibility.

Whitby's Whaling History in the 18th and 19th Centuries

During the 18th and early 19th centuries, Whitby thrived as a whaling port, playing a vital role in the lucrative trade.

- **Growth of the Industry:** Whitby's strategic location along the North Sea and its skilled seafaring population made it a natural hub for whaling. Local ships ventured as far as the Arctic to hunt whales for their blubber, which was processed into oil and used for lamps, soaps, and industrial lubricants.
    - The height of the industry saw fleets of Whitby ships departing annually for long and dangerous voyages.
- **Economic Impact:** Whaling brought prosperity to Whitby, employing large numbers of sailors, coopers, and shipbuilders. The wealth generated from the trade contributed to the growth of the town, funding infrastructure, and expanding its maritime influence.
- **Decline of Whaling:** By the mid-19th century, the advent of petroleum products and the declining whale populations led to the industry's decline. However, its legacy remains etched in Whitby's history and the memories of its people.

How the Arch Became a Symbol of Whitby

The Whalebone Arch has evolved into a symbol that encapsulates Whitby's unique identity.

- **A Tribute to Maritime Heritage:** The arch serves as a tangible link to Whitby's whaling past, reminding visitors of the town's seafaring resilience and its role in global trade. It stands alongside other maritime landmarks, such as the Captain Cook Memorial and the harbor, to celebrate Whitby's storied history.

- **Tourist Attraction and Cultural Icon:** Today, the Whalebone Arch is one of the most photographed spots in Whitby. It attracts tourists for its aesthetic appeal, cultural significance, and stunning views. The juxtaposition of the arch against the ruins of **Whitby Abbey** creates a powerful image that resonates with visitors.
- **Modern Reflection and Conservation Message:** While the arch celebrates Whitby's whaling history, it also prompts reflection on the environmental impact of past industries. The bowhead whale bones used for the current arch were sourced sustainably, representing a modern commitment to conservation.

Why the Whalebone Arch Is a Must-Visit

The Whalebone Arch offers something for everyone:

- **For History Enthusiasts:** It tells the story of Whitby's whaling legacy and maritime achievements.
- **For Photographers:** The arch provides a stunning frame for views of the town, Abbey, and sea.
- **For Environmentalists:** It stands as a reminder of the need for sustainable practices and respect for marine ecosystems.

Final Thoughts

The Whalebone Arch is much more than a decorative structure; it's a gateway to Whitby's rich maritime heritage and a poignant reminder of the town's historical reliance on the sea. By visiting the arch, you connect with Whitby's past, appreciate its cultural symbolism, and witness one of the most beautiful vantage points in this charming coastal town. Whether for its history, its views, or its deeper message, the Whalebone Arch remains an enduring emblem of Whitby's unique identity.

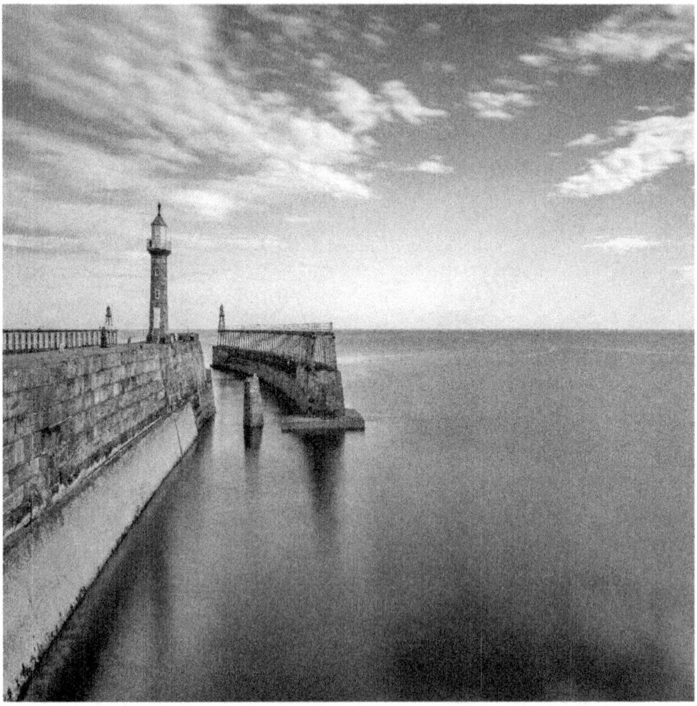

Chapter 4
Beaches and Coastal Adventures

Whitby Beach and West Cliff

Whitby Beach and the adjacent West Cliff area provide an ideal setting for family fun, exploration, and relaxation. From sunbathing and sandcastle building to fossil hunting and romantic sunset strolls, this stretch of coastline offers a perfect mix of natural beauty and seaside activities. In this section, we explore the family-friendly appeal of Whitby Beach, the thrill of fossil hunting at West Cliff, and the tranquil experiences of sunset spots and seaside walks.

Family-Friendly Activities at Whitby Beach

Whitby Beach is a haven for families, offering a wide range of activities that cater to visitors of all ages.

- **Classic Seaside Fun:** The beach's expanse of soft sand and shallow waters is perfect for traditional family activities:
  - **Sandcastle Building:** Children can let their imaginations run wild, crafting elaborate sandcastles and sculptures.
  - **Paddling and Swimming:** The beach is a designated safe swimming zone, with calm waters that are ideal for splashing about. During peak seasons, lifeguards ensure safety for all beachgoers.
  - **Beach Sports:** Frisbee, volleyball, and beach cricket are common sights on sunny days.
- **Whitby's Beach Huts:** Adding a touch of charm, the colorful beach huts lining the promenade are a quintessential part of the Whitby Beach experience. Visitors can rent these huts for the day, offering a private space to relax and enjoy the seaside atmosphere.
- **Amenities and Accessibility:** The beach is equipped with family-friendly facilities, including toilets, changing rooms, and kiosks selling ice cream and

snacks. Accessibility is a priority, with ramps and pathways available for strollers and wheelchairs.

Whitby Beach provides a safe, vibrant, and welcoming environment for families, ensuring a memorable day by the sea.

Fossil Hunting and Rock Pooling at West Cliff

The cliffs and rocky outcrops at West Cliff are a treasure trove of geological and ecological wonders.

- **Fossil Hunting:** As part of the famous Jurassic Coast, Whitby is rich in prehistoric fossils, offering an exciting activity for budding paleontologists and nature lovers alike:
    - **What to Find:** Fossils of ammonites, belemnites, and even marine reptiles have been discovered in the shale cliffs surrounding Whitby.
    - **Where to Look:** The best spots for fossil hunting are at the base of the cliffs, particularly after high tide or heavy rainfall when fresh layers of rock are exposed.
    - **Guided Fossil Tours:** For beginners, guided fossil hunting tours provide expert insights into what to look for and how to do so responsibly.
- **Rock Pooling Adventures:** Exploring the rock pools at low tide reveals a vibrant world of marine life:
    - **Creatures to Discover:** Crabs, starfish, anemones, and small fish can be spotted in the pools, making it a fun and educational activity for children.
    - **Eco-Friendly Exploration:** Visitors are encouraged to tread lightly and leave creatures undisturbed, ensuring that Whitby's coastal ecosystems remain intact for future generations.

The combination of fossil hunting and rock pooling adds an element of discovery to any visit to West Cliff, creating lasting memories for visitors young and old.

Sunset Spots and Seaside Strolls

Whitby's coastline is renowned for its breathtaking sunsets and scenic walking opportunities, providing a peaceful escape for visitors seeking tranquility.

- **Best Sunset Spots:** As the sun dips below the horizon, Whitby's beaches and cliffs are bathed in golden light:
    - **West Cliff Promenade:** Elevated views from the promenade make this one of the best places to watch the sun set over the North Sea. The Whalebone Arch adds a picturesque frame for photos.
    - **Whitby Abbey:** For a more dramatic sunset experience, head to the East Cliff near the Abbey. The silhouette of the Abbey's ruins against the vibrant sky is an unforgettable sight.
    - **Harbor Views:** Watching the sunset from the harbor offers a tranquil setting, with the soft sounds of the waves and fishing boats returning to dock.
- **Seaside Strolls:** Walking along the coastline is a soothing way to take in Whitby's natural beauty:
    - **Promenade Walks:** The paved paths along Whitby Beach are ideal for leisurely strolls, with seating areas to pause and enjoy the views.
    - **Clifftop Trails:** For a more adventurous walk, trails along the cliffs offer panoramic vistas of the coastline and sea. These trails connect to the Cleveland Way, a popular hiking route.
    - **Beach Walks:** At low tide, the expansive sands provide ample space for long walks along the shore, with the rhythmic sound of the waves as a constant companion.
- **Romantic Ambiance:** The combination of stunning sunsets and peaceful walks makes Whitby Beach and West Cliff a favorite spot for couples seeking a romantic escape.

Why Whitby Beach and West Cliff Are Must-Visit Destinations

Whitby Beach and West Cliff offer an ideal blend of family-friendly fun, natural exploration, and serene beauty:

- **For Families:** The safe swimming zones, amenities, and activities ensure an enjoyable experience for all ages.
- **For Nature Enthusiasts:** Fossil hunting and rock pooling provide a unique opportunity to connect with Whitby's natural history.
- **For Scenic Seekers:** The sunsets and walking paths showcase the best of Whitby's picturesque coastline.

Final Thoughts

Whitby Beach and West Cliff are quintessential parts of any visit to Whitby, offering something for everyone. Whether you're building sandcastles with your family, uncovering ancient fossils, or simply watching the sun set over the sea, these coastal gems promise a memorable experience. Embrace the charm of Whitby's beaches and let the soothing rhythm of the waves create memories to last a lifetime.

Sandsend Beach

Sandsend Beach is a picturesque gem just a few miles from Whitby, offering visitors a serene escape with a mix of natural beauty and charming amenities. Known for its tranquil atmosphere, the beach caters to those seeking relaxation, light adventure, and coastal indulgence. This section explores Sandsend Beach as a peaceful retreat, its scenic walking trails to Whitby, and the delightful dining options along its shores.

A Quieter Retreat for Relaxation and Surfing

Unlike the bustling main beach in Whitby, Sandsend Beach provides a quieter, more tranquil experience, making it ideal for visitors looking to unwind.

- **Peaceful Atmosphere:** Sandsend is perfect for relaxation, with its wide expanse of soft sand, gentle waves, and fewer crowds. It's a haven for families,

couples, and solo travelers wanting to enjoy the calming sounds of the sea away from the hustle and bustle.
- **Surfing and Water Activities:**
  - **Surf-Friendly Waters:** The beach's steady waves make it a popular spot for beginner and intermediate surfers. Sandsend has surf schools and equipment rentals for those eager to try their hand at riding the waves.
  - **Paddleboarding and Kayaking:** The calm sections of the water near Sandsend are perfect for paddleboarding and kayaking, offering a mix of exercise and scenic exploration.
- **Seaside Relaxation:** Visitors can bring along deck chairs or beach blankets to soak up the sun or read a book, with the dramatic backdrop of the North Sea and lush cliffs adding to the ambiance.

Sandsend's combination of tranquility and light water sports ensures there's something for everyone, whether they're seeking activity or rest.

Walking Trails Connecting Sandsend to Whitby

Sandsend Beach is also a gateway to some of the most scenic walking trails in the area, including the route that links Sandsend to Whitby.

- **The Coastal Path:** A **two-mile walking trail** along the coastline connects Sandsend to Whitby, offering breathtaking views of the North Sea, rugged cliffs, and sandy shores. The walk is relatively easy and family-friendly, making it suitable for visitors of all fitness levels.
  - **Highlights Along the Way:** The trail passes through sections of beach and clifftop, with opportunities to spot seabirds, explore rock pools, or simply pause and take in the view.
- **The Cleveland Way National Trail:** For more adventurous walkers, Sandsend Beach is part of the famous **Cleveland Way**, a long-distance hiking trail that stretches 109 miles across the Yorkshire coastline and moorlands. This trail provides stunning perspectives of the area's natural beauty and is a favorite for avid hikers.

- **Tidal Awareness:** Walkers should be mindful of the tides, as parts of the route along the beach can become inaccessible during high tide. Maps and tide charts are available locally to help plan your journey.

Walking from Sandsend to Whitby not only offers exercise and fresh sea air but also a deeper appreciation of the region's coastal charm.

Dining Options Along the Sandsend Coast

Sandsend's charm extends beyond its beach and trails to include an array of delightful dining options.

- **Seaside Cafés:**
    - **Estbek House:** This award-winning restaurant is known for its locally sourced ingredients and elegant dishes, including fresh seafood caught along the Yorkshire coast. It offers a fine dining experience in a cozy and historic setting.
    - **Sandsend Café:** A casual spot offering hearty breakfasts, light lunches, and warm drinks. Its outdoor seating area provides stunning sea views, making it an ideal place to relax after a walk or swim.
- **Traditional Pubs:**
    - **The Hart Inn:** This historic pub is a favorite among locals and visitors, offering a warm atmosphere, a wide selection of ales, and a menu filled with classic pub fare like fish and chips, pies, and hearty stews.
- **Ice Cream and Snacks:** Kiosks and small shops along Sandsend Beach provide quick refreshments, including freshly made ice cream, snacks, and cold drinks. These spots are perfect for a casual treat while enjoying the view.
- **Seasonal Dining:** During the warmer months, Sandsend hosts pop-up stalls and food trucks offering everything from seafood dishes to locally made desserts, enhancing the culinary experience for beachgoers.

Dining along the Sandsend coast is not just about great food—it's about savoring the flavors while immersed in the serene seaside atmosphere.

Why Sandsend Beach Is a Must-Visit

Sandsend Beach offers a unique blend of peace, adventure, and coastal charm, making it a standout destination near Whitby:

- **For Relaxation Seekers:** Its quiet ambiance and stunning scenery make it perfect for unwinding.
- **For Walkers:** The trails connecting Sandsend to Whitby provide a rewarding way to explore the coastline.
- **For Food Enthusiasts:** A range of cafés, pubs, and restaurants ensures every palate is satisfied.

Final Thoughts

Sandsend Beach is a hidden treasure on the Yorkshire coast, offering an idyllic escape for visitors seeking tranquility, scenic exploration, and coastal indulgence. Whether you're strolling along the sandy shore, enjoying a hearty meal with sea views, or catching waves on a surfboard, Sandsend promises an experience that refreshes the body and soul. Embrace the slower pace of life at this charming retreat, and discover why Sandsend is a favorite destination for locals and travelers alike.

Boat Trips and Coastal Cruises

Whitby's scenic harbor and surrounding coastline provide the perfect backdrop for boat trips and cruises. These excursions allow visitors to explore the town's maritime heritage, enjoy stunning seascapes, and connect with the natural world. From fishing charters to Dracula-themed evening cruises, Whitby's boat trips offer a range of unique experiences. This section highlights the best options for fishing enthusiasts, literature lovers, and wildlife spotters.

Fishing Charters and Marine Tours

Fishing charters are a longstanding tradition in Whitby, offering visitors the chance to experience the thrill of the town's historic fishing trade firsthand.

- **Traditional Fishing Charters:** Whitby's charter boats cater to anglers of all skill levels, providing everything needed for a successful outing:
  - **Half-Day and Full-Day Trips:** Fishing charters offer flexible options, ranging from brief excursions to full-day adventures. Participants can expect to catch species such as cod, mackerel, and ling, depending on the season.
  - **Expert Guidance:** Local skippers share tips, tricks, and insights into the best fishing spots in the North Sea, ensuring a rewarding experience for beginners and seasoned anglers alike.
- **Family-Friendly Options:** Many charters are tailored to families, making fishing an accessible and enjoyable activity for all ages. Shorter trips with lighter gear are designed to engage children and introduce them to the basics of fishing.
- **Marine Tours:** For those less interested in fishing, marine tours offer a relaxed way to experience Whitby's coastline. These trips often include commentary on the area's maritime history, geology, and wildlife, providing a deeper understanding of the region's significance.

Fishing charters and marine tours are a must for visitors wanting a hands-on connection to Whitby's seafaring traditions.

The Famous Dracula Evening Cruises

Whitby's ties to Bram Stoker's *Dracula* come alive on the **Dracula evening cruises**, a thrilling way to explore the gothic lore that has captivated visitors for over a century.

- **Atmospheric Storytelling:** These evening cruises delve into the chilling tale of *Dracula*, as narrated by local guides. Passengers learn about the famous scenes in Stoker's novel that are set in Whitby, including Dracula's dramatic arrival on the ship *Demeter*.
  - Guides often weave in anecdotes about Whitby's gothic architecture and the town's role in inspiring the novel's eerie tone.

- **Stunning Twilight Views:** The cruises take place as the sun sets over the North Sea, creating an atmospheric backdrop for the storytelling. The darkening sky and glistening waters add to the spine-tingling ambiance.
- **Costumes and Themed Events:** Many Dracula cruises feature costumed actors who enhance the experience with theatrical reenactments. Special themed events during the Whitby Goth Weekend make these cruises even more memorable.

The Dracula evening cruises offer an immersive blend of history, literature, and entertainment, making them a favorite for gothic enthusiasts and casual visitors alike.

Wildlife Spotting from the Sea: Dolphins and Seabirds

For nature lovers, Whitby's boat trips offer unparalleled opportunities to observe marine life and seabirds in their natural habitats.

- **Dolphin Watching:** Dolphins are increasingly spotted off the Yorkshire coast, and many boat tours include wildlife watching as part of their itineraries:
  - **Bottlenose Dolphins:** Pods of playful bottlenose dolphins are a common sight, often seen leaping through the waves alongside boats.
  - **Seasonal Sightings:** Late spring and summer are the best times to spot dolphins, as they follow the migration patterns of fish along the coastline.
- **Seabird Colonies:** The towering cliffs near Whitby are home to diverse seabird species, making boat tours a prime opportunity for birdwatching:
  - **Puffins:** These colorful birds nest along the coast during the breeding season, delighting visitors with their distinctive appearance.
  - **Gannets and Kittiwakes:** Large colonies of these seabirds can be observed soaring over the cliffs and diving into the sea for fish.
- **Eco-Friendly Tours:** Many wildlife tours emphasize sustainable practices, ensuring that the marine environment and its inhabitants remain undisturbed. Guides share information about conservation efforts and encourage responsible observation.

Spotting dolphins and seabirds from the sea provides a magical connection to Whitby's natural beauty and marine biodiversity.

Why Boat Trips and Coastal Cruises Are Essential Experiences

Whitby's boat trips and cruises cater to a wide range of interests:

- **For Fishing Enthusiasts:** Charter boats offer authentic seafaring adventures and a chance to reel in impressive catches.
- **For Literature Fans:** Dracula cruises bring the gothic lore of Whitby to life in a dramatic and engaging way.
- **For Wildlife Lovers:** Dolphin sightings and seabird colonies showcase the thriving ecosystems of the North Sea.

Final Thoughts

Whitby's boat trips and coastal cruises are a highlight of any visit, offering unforgettable experiences on the water. Whether you're casting a line on a fishing charter, embracing the gothic allure of Dracula-themed cruises, or marveling at dolphins and puffins, these excursions promise adventure and wonder. Step aboard, and let Whitby's maritime heritage and natural beauty enchant you.

Chapter 5
Gothic Whitby

Whitby's Gothic Reputation

Whitby's gothic reputation has become an integral part of its identity, drawing literary enthusiasts, gothic culture followers, and curious travelers alike. This dark charm is deeply intertwined with Bram Stoker's *Dracula*, its haunting architecture, and the thriving gothic subculture that calls Whitby home. This section explores how *Dracula* immortalized Whitby's eerie appeal, the town's striking gothic architecture, and the rise of its vibrant gothic community.

How Dracula Popularized Whitby's Dark Charm

The gothic allure of Whitby owes much of its fame to Bram Stoker's 1897 novel *Dracula*.

- **Stoker's Visit to Whitby:** Bram Stoker visited Whitby in 1890, staying at a guesthouse on the West Cliff. The town's rugged coastline, dramatic Abbey ruins, and brooding atmosphere left a lasting impression on him. These elements would later inspire key scenes in his novel.
- **Dracula's Arrival in Whitby:** In *Dracula*, the Count arrives in England aboard the doomed ship *Demeter*, which crashes onto Whitby's shores during a storm. The scene is vividly set against the backdrop of the East Cliff and the Abbey ruins, capturing the eerie mood that Whitby naturally evokes. The dramatic imagery of Dracula's transformation into a dog and leaping onto the land has cemented Whitby as a quintessential gothic setting.
- **Literary Legacy:** Stoker's novel elevated Whitby's status as a gothic destination. Fans of *Dracula* flock to the town to retrace the story's steps, from the harbor to the Abbey and the graveyard of St. Mary's Church. The enduring appeal of Stoker's masterpiece has firmly placed Whitby on the map as a literary and gothic landmark.

Gothic Architecture and Its Presence in Whitby

Whitby's gothic appeal is not limited to its literary connections. Its architecture amplifies the dark and mysterious atmosphere that visitors find so enchanting.

- **Whitby Abbey:** The towering ruins of Whitby Abbey are the epitome of gothic grandeur. Built in the 13th century in the Early English Gothic style, the Abbey's pointed arches, intricate stone carvings, and weathered appearance create a dramatic silhouette against the sky. The Abbey's cliffside location adds to its ominous allure, particularly at twilight or during misty mornings.
- **St. Mary's Church and Graveyard:** Perched near the Abbey, **St. Mary's Church** is another example of gothic influence in Whitby. Its graveyard, filled with weathered headstones and overlooking the harbor, is famously associated with *Dracula*. The setting provides a classic gothic atmosphere, blending history, decay, and natural beauty.
- **The Whalebone Arch and Piers:** While not strictly gothic in design, landmarks like the **Whalebone Arch** and Whitby's piers contribute to the dramatic coastal scenery that enhances the town's mystique.
- **Gothic Details Throughout the Town:** From narrow cobblestone streets to historic inns and Victorian-era shopfronts, Whitby's architectural landscape is filled with elements that evoke a gothic aesthetic. Even modern businesses often adopt the theme, further embedding it into the town's identity.

The Rise of Whitby's Gothic Subculture

The gothic reputation sparked by *Dracula* has grown into a thriving subculture, with Whitby now serving as a focal point for gothic enthusiasts from around the world.

- **Whitby Goth Weekend (WGW):** First held in 1994, the **Whitby Goth Weekend** has become one of the UK's most renowned gothic festivals.
    - **What to Expect:** The event includes live music, fashion shows, and themed markets, drawing thousands of attendees dressed in gothic attire

ranging from Victorian-inspired ensembles to contemporary punk influences.
- **Community Connection:** WGW celebrates not only gothic style but also the camaraderie of its participants, creating a welcoming space for self-expression.
- **Year-Round Gothic Influence:** Beyond the festival, Whitby embraces its gothic identity year-round. Shops sell gothic clothing, accessories, and literature, while cafés and pubs often host themed events. The town's tourism industry caters to gothic enthusiasts with Dracula tours, ghost walks, and themed accommodations.
- **Art and Music:** Whitby's gothic subculture extends into the arts, with local galleries showcasing dark, atmospheric works inspired by the town. Music venues often host performances by gothic bands, further enriching the scene.

Why Whitby's Gothic Reputation Is Unmissable

Whitby's gothic allure offers something for everyone:

- **For Literature Lovers:** The connections to *Dracula* provide an opportunity to delve into one of gothic literature's most iconic works.
- **For Architecture Aficionados:** The town's historic buildings and ruins showcase the timeless appeal of gothic design.
- **For Gothic Culture Enthusiasts:** Events like Whitby Goth Weekend and the town's year-round offerings make it a hub for celebrating gothic fashion, art, and music.

Final Thoughts

Whitby's gothic reputation is a blend of literary heritage, striking architecture, and a vibrant subculture that continues to grow. From the pages of *Dracula* to the dramatic ruins of Whitby Abbey, the town's dark charm has captured the imagination of visitors for over a century. Whether exploring its eerie landmarks or immersing yourself in the gothic community, Whitby offers an unforgettable experience that celebrates the beauty of the macabre.

Whitby Goth Weekend

The **Whitby Goth Weekend (WGW)** is a world-renowned festival that celebrates gothic culture, creativity, and camaraderie. This biannual event has grown from a small gathering to one of the most significant alternative festivals in the UK. Attracting visitors of all ages and interests, WGW features parades, fashion shows, live music, and more, making it a unique highlight of Whitby's cultural calendar. This section explores the festival's origins, its main attractions, and tips for visitors who want to participate or spectate.

Origins and Growth of This Unique Festival

The Whitby Goth Weekend was founded in 1994 by Jo Hampshire, a fan of gothic music and fashion.

- **The First Gathering:** Initially, the event was a small meeting of like-minded individuals who shared a love for alternative music and the gothic aesthetic. The location was chosen due to Whitby's ties to Bram Stoker's *Dracula*, which had already established the town as a gothic landmark.
- **Expansion Over the Years:** The event grew steadily, attracting a diverse crowd of goth enthusiasts, from traditional Victorian goths to steampunk and punk-inspired attendees.
  - Over the years, it evolved into a biannual festival held in spring and autumn, drawing thousands of participants and spectators from around the world.
  - The festival now encompasses the entire town, with events and activities spread across multiple venues, including the iconic Whitby Pavilion.
- **Global Recognition:** Today, WGW is regarded as one of the most important gothic festivals globally, offering a welcoming environment for alternative subcultures and fostering a strong sense of community.

Highlights: Parades, Fashion Shows, and Music Events

Whitby Goth Weekend is packed with activities and attractions, each showcasing the creativity and diversity of the gothic scene.

- **Parades and Street Style:**
  - The festival's streets come alive with attendees dressed in elaborate gothic, steampunk, and Victorian-inspired outfits. The spontaneous parades and street gatherings provide an informal yet mesmerizing display of fashion.
  - Professional photographers and visitors alike flock to capture these striking visuals, turning Whitby's cobbled streets into a runway of alternative style.
- **Fashion Shows:**
  - Organized fashion shows highlight gothic designers, from intricate corsets and flowing gowns to edgy leatherwear and dramatic accessories. These events often celebrate both established and emerging designers within the gothic community.
  - The shows take place at prominent venues like the Whitby Pavilion and feature models from within the community, creating a truly inclusive atmosphere.
- **Live Music Events:**
  - Music is at the heart of WGW, with performances from gothic, punk, industrial, and alternative bands. The Whitby Pavilion hosts headline acts, while smaller venues across town showcase up-and-coming artists.
  - Genres include everything from classic goth rock and darkwave to industrial beats and ethereal melodies, ensuring something for every music enthusiast.
- **Alternative Markets:**
  - Stalls and markets offer unique goods, including gothic clothing, handcrafted jewelry, alternative art, and themed souvenirs. These markets are perfect for finding one-of-a-kind items that reflect the festival's spirit.

How Visitors Can Participate or Spectate

Whitby Goth Weekend is an inclusive event, welcoming participants and spectators alike. Whether you're fully immersed in gothic culture or simply curious, there are plenty of ways to engage with the festival.

- **Participating in the Festival:**
  - **Dress the Part:** While not mandatory, dressing in gothic or alternative fashion enhances the experience. Attendees often put months of effort into crafting intricate outfits that reflect their individuality.
  - **Attend Events:** Purchase tickets for music performances, fashion shows, and other official events to immerse yourself in the festival's core activities. Advance booking is recommended for popular shows at the Whitby Pavilion.
  - **Join the Community:** Engage with fellow attendees, join informal gatherings, and participate in photo sessions. The festival is a fantastic opportunity to meet people who share similar interests.
- **Spectating the Festival:**
  - **Strolling Through Town:** Many festival activities take place outdoors, making it easy for spectators to enjoy the vibrant atmosphere without committing to ticketed events.
  - **Explore Markets and Stalls:** Visit the gothic markets to browse and shop for unique items, even if you're not dressed in gothic attire.
  - **Capture the Magic:** Bring your camera to document the incredible outfits, parades, and energy of the festival. Be respectful and ask for permission before taking close-up photos of attendees.
- **Practical Tips for Visitors:**
  - **Plan Ahead:** Accommodation in Whitby fills up quickly during WGW. Book your stay well in advance or consider staying in nearby towns like Scarborough or Robin Hood's Bay.

- ➤ **Check the Schedule:** Official schedules are published on the festival's website and social media channels, helping you plan your experience and avoid missing key events.
- ➤ **Enjoy the Atmosphere:** Even if you're not attending specific events, simply being in Whitby during the Goth Weekend is an experience in itself, as the entire town transforms into a gothic wonderland.

Why Whitby Goth Weekend Is a Must-Experience

Whitby Goth Weekend is more than a festival—it's a celebration of creativity, individuality, and community.

- **For Gothic Enthusiasts:** It's an opportunity to express yourself, connect with like-minded individuals, and celebrate gothic culture in a historic and atmospheric setting.
- **For Spectators:** The festival's visual spectacle and welcoming vibe make it an unforgettable experience, even for those new to the gothic scene.
- **For Whitby Lovers:** WGW enhances the charm of this seaside town, blending its rich history with the vibrant energy of modern subcultures.

Final Thoughts

Whitby Goth Weekend is a unique festival that embodies the spirit of gothic culture while paying homage to Whitby's literary and architectural heritage. Whether you're participating in elaborate fashion parades, enjoying live music, or simply soaking in the atmospheric streets, WGW promises an unforgettable experience for all. It's a testament to Whitby's enduring ability to inspire and connect people through its gothic charm.

Gothic Shopping and Art

Whitby is a haven for gothic enthusiasts, with its charming cobbled streets and historic alleys filled with specialty shops and galleries. Visitors can find unique treasures, from elaborate gothic fashion and Dracula-inspired artwork to thoughtful souvenirs that capture Whitby's dark allure. This section explores the town's gothic shopping scene, its art galleries showcasing gothic themes, and the best keepsakes for fans of the macabre.

Specialty Shops Selling Gothic Fashion and Accessories

Whitby's shopping experience is tailored to gothic culture, offering a variety of stores that cater to every aesthetic and interest.

- **Gothic Clothing and Accessories:**
    - **Alternative Fashion Boutiques:** Whitby is home to several shops specializing in gothic clothing, such as corsets, lace dresses, leather jackets, and tailored coats.
    - **Jewelry and Accessories:** Many boutiques offer gothic-inspired jewelry, including chokers, rings, and brooches adorned with skulls, bats, and crosses. These pieces often feature materials like Whitby jet, a black gemstone locally sourced and historically tied to mourning jewelry.
- **Notable Shops:**
    - **Pandemonium:** A favorite among gothic fashion lovers, this shop offers a curated collection of gothic and steampunk attire.
    - **Sutcliffe Gallery:** Renowned for its exquisite jet jewelry, it combines tradition with gothic style, making it a must-visit for those seeking unique accessories.
    - **Black Market:** Located in Whitby's heart, this shop caters to alternative subcultures, with clothing, home décor, and gifts that reflect the gothic lifestyle.

Whitby's shops seamlessly blend local history with modern gothic trends, creating an unparalleled shopping experience.

Art Galleries Showcasing Gothic and Dracula-Inspired Works

For art lovers, Whitby's gothic influence extends into its vibrant art scene, with galleries displaying pieces inspired by the town's dark charm.

- **Dracula and Gothic-Inspired Art:**
  - Local artists frequently draw inspiration from Whitby's ties to Bram Stoker's *Dracula* and its atmospheric landscapes. Paintings and illustrations often feature Whitby Abbey, the Whalebone Arch, and stormy coastal scenes with a haunting aesthetic.
- **Sculpture and Crafts:**
  - Gothic sculptures, including gargoyles, abstract pieces, and handcrafted figurines, are popular offerings in Whitby's art galleries.
- **Notable Galleries:**
  - **The Whitby Galleries:** Located on Church Street, this gallery features a range of gothic and alternative art, from dramatic coastal paintings to Dracula-inspired pieces.
  - **Inspired by... Gallery:** Situated in the nearby North York Moors National Park, this gallery frequently exhibits work from artists who celebrate the eerie beauty of Whitby and its surrounding landscapes.

These galleries provide a unique window into how Whitby's gothic heritage continues to inspire creativity and artistic expression.

Souvenirs to Bring Home for Gothic Enthusiasts

Whitby's shops and markets are brimming with souvenirs that capture the essence of its gothic appeal.

- **Dracula Memorabilia:**
  - Fans of Bram Stoker's *Dracula* will find an array of themed items, including books, posters, and figurines of Count Dracula. Many shops also sell *Dracula*-inspired home décor, such as candles, mugs, and wall art.
- **Whitby Jet Jewelry:**
  - As one of Whitby's most famous exports, jet jewelry makes for an elegant and meaningful keepsake. Necklaces, earrings, and bracelets crafted from this glossy black gemstone are deeply tied to Whitby's history and gothic culture.

- **Gothic Accessories:**
    - Items like pocket watches, Victorian-style parasols, and leather-bound journals reflect the gothic aesthetic while serving as practical mementos.
- **Local Crafts and Décor:**
    - Shops also sell handcrafted goods, such as gothic-themed ceramics, candleholders, and wall hangings, perfect for adding a touch of Whitby's dark charm to any home.

For gothic enthusiasts, these souvenirs offer a way to bring a piece of Whitby's unique character into their daily lives.

Why Gothic Shopping and Art Are Must-Experience Activities

Whitby's gothic shopping and art scene is a highlight for visitors, offering unique treasures that embody the town's atmosphere:

- **For Fashion Lovers:** Specialty shops cater to a range of gothic styles, from Victorian elegance to steampunk edge.
- **For Art Enthusiasts:** Galleries showcase the creativity inspired by Whitby's haunting beauty and literary heritage.
- **For Souvenir Seekers:** Thoughtfully crafted keepsakes ensure you can carry a piece of Whitby's gothic spirit home with you.

Final Thoughts

Whitby's gothic shopping and art offer a captivating blend of history, creativity, and culture. From browsing boutiques filled with dramatic fashion to admiring Dracula-inspired artwork in galleries, the experience is as immersive as it is memorable. Whether you're searching for the perfect jet accessory, a piece of gothic décor, or a striking work of art, Whitby's gothic treasures ensure you'll leave with more than just memories.

Chapter 6
Food and Drink in Whitby

Local Seafood and Fish and Chips

Whitby's culinary landscape is synonymous with seafood, and the town has earned an exceptional reputation for serving some of the best fish and chips in the UK. Beyond this iconic dish, Whitby's seafood restaurants and takeaway spots offer a variety of fresh, locally sourced delicacies. Coupled with a focus on sustainability, the fishing industry ensures that Whitby's coastal charm is matched by its commitment to preserving marine resources. This section explores Whitby's fame for fish and chips, its celebrated seafood establishments, and the role of sustainable fishing in maintaining its culinary traditions.

Whitby's Reputation for the Best Fish and Chips

Whitby's fish and chips have long been celebrated as some of the finest in the country, a claim backed by generations of locals and visitors alike.

- **History of Fish and Chips in Whitby:** The tradition of serving fish and chips in Whitby dates back to the early 20th century, when the town's fishing industry flourished. Local fishermen supplied the freshest fish, which was fried and paired with crispy golden chips for a simple yet delicious meal. Over the years, Whitby's fish and chip shops have become a staple for visitors.
- **Why They're the Best:**
    - **Freshness:** Whitby's location on the North Sea ensures a steady supply of high-quality fish, particularly haddock, which is the preferred choice in the region.
    - **Technique:** The fish is typically coated in a light, crisp batter and fried to perfection, ensuring a golden exterior while preserving the tender, flaky texture inside.
    - **Seaside Setting:** Enjoying fish and chips with a view of Whitby's harbor or Abbey adds an unforgettable charm to the experience.

- **Awards and Recognition:** Several establishments in Whitby have won awards for their fish and chips, further solidifying the town's culinary reputation.

Renowned Seafood Restaurants and Takeaway Spots

Whitby is home to an array of seafood establishments, ranging from traditional takeaways to fine-dining restaurants, ensuring there's something for everyone.

- **Top Fish and Chip Shops:**
  - **The Magpie Café:** Known nationwide, this iconic spot has been serving fish and chips for decades. The Magpie offers both takeaway and dine-in options, with an extensive seafood menu alongside its classic haddock and chips.
  - **Trenchers:** Another award-winning eatery, Trenchers is celebrated for its generous portions, perfectly fried fish, and welcoming atmosphere.
  - **Quayside:** Located near the harbor, Quayside is famous for its locally sourced fish, cooked in traditional beef dripping for an authentic flavor.
- **Seafood Restaurants:**
  - **The Star Inn the Harbour:** This fine-dining restaurant offers an elevated seafood experience, featuring dishes like grilled lobster, mussels, and scallops, paired with stunning views of the harbor.
  - **Hadley's Fish Restaurant:** A classic choice for families, Hadley's combines great service with a menu showcasing a variety of seafood dishes, including prawn cocktails and seafood platters.
- **Local Takeaways:** For a quick bite, many takeaways around the harbor serve freshly cooked fish and chips wrapped in paper, perfect for enjoying while strolling along the promenade.

Whitby's seafood scene strikes a balance between tradition and innovation, satisfying both casual diners and gourmet enthusiasts.

Sustainability and Local Fishing Practices

Whitby's fishing industry has adapted over the years to prioritize sustainability and environmental stewardship.

- **Locally Sourced Seafood:** The majority of seafood served in Whitby is caught locally, ensuring freshness while supporting the town's fishing community. Haddock, cod, crab, and lobster are the most commonly harvested species.
- **Sustainable Practices:**
  - **Fishing Quotas:** Whitby's fishermen adhere to strict quotas and regulations to prevent overfishing and maintain healthy fish populations.
  - **Responsible Techniques:** The use of sustainable fishing gear and methods minimizes environmental impact and ensures that marine habitats remain intact.
- **Supporting Local Fishermen:** By sourcing seafood directly from local fishermen, Whitby's restaurants and fish markets play a vital role in preserving the town's maritime economy.
- **Community Involvement:** Visitors can support sustainability efforts by choosing restaurants and shops that prioritize eco-friendly practices. Many establishments proudly display their commitment to responsible sourcing, making it easy for diners to make informed choices.

Sustainability not only ensures the long-term health of marine ecosystems but also preserves the legacy of Whitby's seafood industry for future generations.

Why Local Seafood and Fish and Chips Are Must-Try Experiences

Whitby's culinary heritage offers more than just a meal; it's an immersive experience that reflects the town's maritime roots and community spirit.

- **For Foodies:** The quality, flavor, and diversity of seafood in Whitby make it a dream destination for lovers of fresh, authentic cuisine.

- **For Families:** The abundance of casual, family-friendly establishments ensures that everyone can enjoy a classic fish and chips feast.
- **For Eco-Conscious Travelers:** Supporting Whitby's sustainable seafood industry allows visitors to contribute to the town's environmental and economic well-being.

Final Thoughts

Whitby's reputation as a seafood haven is well-earned, with its fish and chips standing as a national treasure. Whether dining at a renowned restaurant, enjoying a takeaway by the harbor, or learning about the sustainable practices behind the scenes, visitors are sure to savor every bite. The marriage of tradition, flavor, and responsibility ensures that Whitby's seafood offerings remain an essential part of its charm, inviting travelers to return time and again for a taste of the sea.

Traditional Yorkshire Cuisine

Whitby offers more than just its famous seafood; it is also a gateway to the hearty and flavorful cuisine of Yorkshire. From savory classics like Yorkshire pudding to sweet treats like parkin, the town's culinary landscape reflects the rich traditions of the region. Visitors can enjoy these dishes in welcoming pubs, discover fresh local produce at farmers' markets, and celebrate Yorkshire's culinary heritage at food festivals. This section explores must-try dishes, local pubs serving regional fare, and opportunities to experience Yorkshire's food culture firsthand.

Must-Try Dishes: Yorkshire Pudding, Parkin, and More

Yorkshire's traditional cuisine is characterized by simple, hearty ingredients transformed into comforting dishes.

- **Yorkshire Pudding:** No discussion of Yorkshire cuisine would be complete without mentioning this iconic dish. Made from a batter of eggs, flour, and milk, Yorkshire pudding is a versatile staple served with Sunday roasts. In Whitby, you'll find it paired with gravy or filled with savory stews for a satisfying meal.

- **Parkin:**
  This traditional ginger cake is a beloved treat in Yorkshire. Made with oats, treacle, and ginger, parkin has a rich, moist texture and a spicy-sweet flavor. It's particularly popular in autumn and is often enjoyed with a cup of tea.
- **Whitby Lemon Buns:** A local specialty, these sweet buns are soft and tangy, topped with a delicate glaze. They're a must-try for those seeking a uniquely Whitby twist on Yorkshire desserts.
- **Wensleydale Cheese:** Produced in nearby Wensleydale, this creamy and crumbly cheese pairs beautifully with fruitcake or crackers. Many restaurants and shops in Whitby incorporate it into their menus, making it an essential taste of the region.
- **Meat and Game Dishes:** Yorkshire is known for its high-quality meat and game, including dishes like steak and ale pie, venison stew, and lamb shank. Locally sourced ingredients ensure that these meals are both fresh and flavorful.

Pubs Offering Hearty Local Fare

Traditional Yorkshire cuisine is best experienced in the warm and inviting atmosphere of Whitby's pubs.

- **The Black Horse Inn:** One of Whitby's oldest pubs, the Black Horse Inn offers a menu filled with regional classics, including Yorkshire pudding served with roast beef and rich, gravy-laden pies. Its rustic charm and history make it a favorite among locals and visitors alike.
- **The White Horse & Griffin:** Known for its blend of tradition and creativity, this pub serves dishes like braised lamb shoulder with seasonal vegetables and treacle sponge for dessert. Its historic building adds to the authentic experience.
- **The Duke of York:** Located near Whitby Harbor, this pub specializes in hearty meals like steak and ale pie, pork sausages with mash, and sticky toffee pudding. Its location provides stunning views to complement the excellent food.

- **The Magpie Café:** While primarily famous for seafood, the Magpie Café also serves Yorkshire staples such as parkin and Wensleydale cheese platters, ensuring there's something for every palate.

These pubs offer the perfect setting to enjoy traditional dishes alongside local ales or ciders, enhancing the overall Yorkshire experience.

Farmers' Markets and Food Festivals

Whitby's vibrant food scene extends beyond its restaurants and pubs to include markets and festivals that showcase the best of local produce and culinary craftsmanship.

- **Farmers' Markets:**
  - **Whitby Farmers' Market:** Held monthly, this market is a treasure trove of locally sourced ingredients, including fresh vegetables, meats, cheeses, and baked goods. It's an excellent opportunity to meet local producers and sample their creations.
  - **Malton Food Lovers Market:** A short drive from Whitby, this renowned market offers a wide range of Yorkshire specialties, from artisanal bread to handcrafted chocolate.
- **Food Festivals:**
  - **Whitby Traction Engine Rally:** This annual event combines history and gastronomy, featuring stalls that offer everything from Yorkshire sausages to sweet treats like fudge and parkin.
  - **Whitby Fish & Ships Festival:** Celebrating Whitby's maritime heritage, this festival also highlights regional cuisine, with vendors offering seafood dishes alongside traditional Yorkshire fare.
  - **Great Yorkshire Show:** While held outside Whitby, this county-wide event showcases the best of Yorkshire's food and drink, making it worth a visit for food enthusiasts.
- **Cooking Classes and Workshops:** Some local establishments offer workshops where visitors can learn to prepare classic Yorkshire dishes, such as baking their own parkin or mastering the art of the perfect Yorkshire pudding.

Why Traditional Yorkshire Cuisine Is a Must-Try in Whitby

Whitby provides the perfect setting to experience Yorkshire's rich culinary traditions.

- **For Food Enthusiasts:** The combination of savory and sweet dishes reflects the diversity of Yorkshire's flavors.
- **For Families:** Hearty meals in welcoming pubs ensure that visitors of all ages leave satisfied.
- **For Cultural Explorers:** Farmers' markets and food festivals offer an authentic glimpse into the region's agricultural and culinary heritage.

Final Thoughts

Whitby's embrace of traditional Yorkshire cuisine adds another layer to its charm. From savoring a plate of roast beef and Yorkshire pudding at a cozy pub to discovering local delicacies at a farmers' market, there's no shortage of opportunities to indulge in the region's rich flavors. Whether you're sampling sweet parkin or enjoying a hearty meat pie, Whitby's food scene is a celebration of Yorkshire's culinary identity.

Whitby's Café and Pub Scene

Whitby's café and pub scene is a blend of cozy charm, historic significance, and a commitment to showcasing local flavors. Whether indulging in homemade desserts at a quaint café, enjoying a pint at a historic pub, or sampling locally brewed ales and craft gin, Whitby offers an unforgettable culinary experience. This section highlights the town's vibrant café culture, the stories behind its historic pubs, and the rise of local distilleries.

Cozy Cafés with Homemade Desserts

Whitby's cafés are celebrated for their welcoming ambiance and an array of delightful treats that cater to all tastes.

- **Homemade Cakes and Bakes:** Many of Whitby's cafés pride themselves on serving freshly made desserts, often using locally sourced ingredients:

- **Whitby Lemon Buns:** Unique to the area, these soft, citrusy buns are a must-try and are available at numerous cafés across town.
    - **Victoria Sponge and Parkin:** Traditional Yorkshire desserts, including ginger-spiced parkin and fluffy sponge cakes, are staples of Whitby's café menus.
    - **Seasonal Specials:** During colder months, many establishments offer comforting treats like sticky toffee pudding or spiced apple cake.
- **Popular Café Spots:**
    - **Sandgate Coffee & Delights:** Known for its specialty coffee and indulgent brownies, this café is a favorite for locals and visitors alike.
    - **Botham's of Whitby:** A historic tearoom and bakery offering a range of traditional Yorkshire desserts, paired with expertly brewed tea.
    - **The Blitz Café:** With its 1940s-inspired decor, this café not only serves delicious cakes but also provides a nostalgic dining experience.
- **A Place to Unwind:** Whitby's cafés provide the perfect setting to relax after exploring the town, with many offering harbor views or cozy interiors that encourage leisurely conversations over coffee and cake.

Historic Pubs and Their Unique Stories

Whitby's historic pubs are not just places to eat and drink—they're windows into the town's rich maritime and cultural history.

- **Centuries of Heritage:** Many of Whitby's pubs have stood for centuries, serving sailors, locals, and travelers. They often retain their original features, from wooden beams to stone fireplaces, creating an authentic atmosphere:
    - **The Endeavour:** Named after Captain Cook's famous ship, this pub celebrates Whitby's maritime heritage with its nautical decor and hearty pub fare.
    - **The Duke of York:** Overlooking the harbor, this pub has long been a gathering place for fishermen. Its walls are adorned with historical photographs and memorabilia.

- ➤ **The Board Inn:** Dating back to the 17th century, this pub offers panoramic views of the harbor and a cozy spot to enjoy a pint.
- **Stories and Legends:** Many of Whitby's pubs are steeped in folklore, with tales of smugglers, ghostly sightings, and historic events. These stories add a layer of intrigue and charm to every visit.
- **Live Music and Community Events:** Several pubs host live music nights, bringing together locals and tourists to enjoy traditional folk tunes and modern performances in a lively setting.

Local Ales and Gin Distilleries

Whitby's commitment to local flavors extends to its drink offerings, with a thriving scene of local ales and craft spirits.

- **Local Breweries:**
  - ➤ **Whitby Brewery:** Situated near Whitby Abbey, this brewery crafts small-batch ales that reflect the character of the town. Popular choices include the golden **Jet Black** and the pale ale **Saltwick Nab**. Visitors can enjoy tastings in the brewery's taproom, which offers stunning views of the Abbey.
  - ➤ **North Yorkshire Brews:** Many pubs and bars in Whitby also serve ales from neighboring breweries, ensuring a diverse selection of regional beers.
- **Craft Gin Distilleries:**
  - ➤ **Whitby Gin:** This award-winning distillery has gained fame for its handcrafted gins, inspired by the local coastline and botanicals. Flavors like **The Bramble & Bay** and **The Original Edition** showcase a balance of tradition and creativity. Tours of the distillery offer insights into the gin-making process, along with tastings.
  - ➤ **Seasonal Specials:** Whitby Gin frequently releases limited-edition flavors that capture the essence of the region, making them popular souvenirs for visitors.
- **Pairing Drinks with Food:** Many pubs and restaurants in Whitby create menus that pair local ales and gins with their dishes, enhancing the dining

experience. From a refreshing gin cocktail with fresh seafood to a robust ale alongside a steak and ale pie, these pairings highlight the best of Whitby's culinary offerings.

Why Whitby's Café and Pub Scene Is Worth Exploring

Whitby's café and pub scene offers something for every visitor:

- **For Sweet Treat Lovers:** Cozy cafés serve some of the best homemade desserts, from traditional Yorkshire parkin to unique Whitby Lemon Buns.
- **For History Enthusiasts:** The town's historic pubs provide a fascinating glimpse into Whitby's maritime past and local legends.
- **For Beverage Connoisseurs:** Local ales and craft gins showcase Whitby's innovative approach to traditional drinks, ensuring a memorable tasting experience.

Final Thoughts

Whitby's cafés and pubs are more than just places to eat and drink—they're an essential part of the town's charm and culture. Whether you're savoring a slice of homemade cake in a cozy café, learning about local history in a centuries-old pub, or sampling award-winning gin, Whitby's café and pub scene offers a rich and satisfying experience. It's the perfect way to indulge, relax, and immerse yourself in the flavors of this enchanting coastal town.

Chapter 7
Outdoor Adventures

Walking and Hiking Trails

Whitby is a walker's paradise, offering an array of trails that showcase its stunning coastline, charming villages, and surrounding countryside. Whether you're an avid hiker seeking a challenge or a family looking for an easy stroll, there's a path for everyone. This section explores the iconic Cleveland Way, the scenic trails linking Whitby to Robin Hood's Bay, and family-friendly walks that make the most of Whitby's natural beauty.

The Cleveland Way: Coastal Beauty on Foot

The **Cleveland Way National Trail** is one of the UK's most scenic long-distance paths, stretching 109 miles through the North York Moors National Park and along the Yorkshire coast. Whitby is a key highlight along the route, making it an ideal starting point for exploring its coastal stretches.

- **Highlights of the Cleveland Way Near Whitby:**
    - **Whitby to Sandsend:** This 3-mile section offers breathtaking views of the North Sea, dramatic cliffs, and sandy beaches. It's a manageable route for walkers of all levels, with a mix of coastal paths and quiet village roads.
    - **Whitby to Robin Hood's Bay:** A longer 7-mile stretch, this part of the trail follows the coastline south, revealing hidden coves, rugged cliffs, and the picturesque village of Robin Hood's Bay.
- **What Makes It Special:**
    - The Cleveland Way combines natural beauty with cultural heritage. Walkers can enjoy panoramic views of the sea, encounter wildlife like seabirds and seals, and explore landmarks like Whitby Abbey and Saltwick Bay.
    - It's perfect for photographers, with ever-changing scenery that includes cliffs, beaches, and quaint villages.
- **Tips for Walkers:**

- Wear sturdy shoes and bring a map or GPS, as parts of the trail involve uneven terrain.
- Check weather conditions before setting out, as coastal winds can be strong.
- Pack water and snacks, especially for longer sections.

For those seeking a challenging yet rewarding outdoor adventure, the Cleveland Way is a must.

Trails Connecting Whitby to Robin Hood's Bay

The trail linking **Whitby and Robin Hood's Bay** is one of the most popular routes for visitors, offering a mix of historical intrigue and natural splendor.

- **The Route:**
    - This 7-mile path starts in Whitby, passing landmarks like the Whalebone Arch and Whitby Abbey before following the Cleveland Way along the coastline.
    - The trail features a combination of cliff-top paths, wooded sections, and rolling fields, providing a variety of landscapes to enjoy.
- **Highlights Along the Way:**
    - **Saltwick Bay:** Known for its fossils and dramatic rock formations, Saltwick Bay is a great spot for a short detour.
    - **Ravenscar:** This quaint village, situated on a high cliff, offers stunning views and is an excellent rest point for walkers.
    - **Robin Hood's Bay:** The trail ends in this charming fishing village, where narrow cobbled streets and a welcoming pub scene await.
- **Wildlife and Scenery:**
    - Walkers can spot seabirds, wildflowers, and even seals along this coastal stretch. The trail's elevation provides sweeping views of the North Sea and the Yorkshire coastline.
- **Planning the Walk:**

- The route takes about 3-4 hours to complete at a moderate pace. For those not up for the return journey on foot, local buses run between Whitby and Robin Hood's Bay.
- Make sure to bring a camera, as the trail offers some of the most iconic views in the region.

Easy Walks for Families with Children

Whitby also caters to families with a variety of shorter, easy-to-navigate trails that allow children to enjoy the outdoors without feeling overwhelmed.

- **The West Cliff Promenade Walk:**
  - This gentle, paved path is ideal for families with strollers or young children. Starting near the Whalebone Arch, the promenade offers stunning views of the beach and harbor below.
  - There are benches along the way for rest stops, and plenty of nearby cafés for a post-walk treat.
- **Pannett Park Nature Trail:**
  - Located in the heart of Whitby, **Pannett Park** is perfect for a leisurely family stroll. The park features well-maintained paths, a play area for kids, and a lovely garden filled with seasonal blooms.
  - Educational signs along the nature trail teach children about local flora and fauna, making it an enjoyable and informative outing.
- **Whitby to Sandsend Beach Walk:**
  - This 3-mile stretch along the beach at low tide is both flat and scenic, making it an excellent choice for families.
  - Kids will enjoy spotting shells and sea creatures, building sandcastles, or simply splashing in the waves. Sandsend itself has a playground and ice cream shops, making it a rewarding endpoint.
- **Tips for Family Walks:**
  - Bring water, snacks, and sunscreen, as some trails may lack shaded areas.
  - Wear comfortable footwear suitable for sand or uneven paths.

- Check tide times for beach walks to ensure a safe and enjoyable experience.

Why Whitby's Walking and Hiking Trails Are a Must-Do

Whitby's walking and hiking trails offer something for every outdoor enthusiast:

- **For Adventurers:** The Cleveland Way provides a challenging yet rewarding experience with unparalleled coastal views.
- **For Explorers:** The trail to Robin Hood's Bay combines history, natural beauty, and the charm of Yorkshire's villages.
- **For Families:** Easy, child-friendly walks ensure that everyone, regardless of age, can enjoy Whitby's great outdoors.

Final Thoughts

Whitby's walking and hiking trails are a testament to the area's stunning natural beauty and rich heritage. From the dramatic cliffs of the Cleveland Way to the family-friendly promenades and beach routes, there's a trail for every interest and ability. Whether you're seeking adventure, relaxation, or a bit of both, Whitby's trails promise an unforgettable experience surrounded by the best that Yorkshire's coast has to offer.

Cycling and Horse Riding

Whitby's stunning landscapes, with their mix of coastal cliffs, verdant moorlands, and winding country paths, are perfect for outdoor activities like cycling and horseback riding. Whether you're pedaling along scenic routes or exploring the countryside on horseback, these activities offer a unique way to immerse yourself in the natural beauty of Yorkshire. This section covers the best cycling paths, horseback riding tours, and practical tips for renting gear and booking guided tours.

Cycle Paths Along the Coast and Through Moorlands

Whitby offers a variety of cycling routes that cater to all skill levels, from leisurely coastal rides to challenging moorland trails.

- **The Cinder Track:**
    - **Overview:** This 21-mile route stretches from Whitby to Scarborough, following a disused railway line. The path is relatively flat and well-maintained, making it suitable for families and beginner cyclists.
    - **Highlights:** Cyclists are treated to breathtaking views of the Yorkshire coastline, quaint villages like Robin Hood's Bay, and peaceful woodlands. It's a perfect way to experience the region's natural beauty without the strain of steep climbs.
- **Moorland Rides:**
    - **Esk Valley Cycle Route:** For those seeking a more challenging adventure, the Esk Valley Cycle Route offers a mix of on-road and off-road trails through the North York Moors National Park.
    - **Scenic Views:** The route is characterized by rolling hills, heather-covered moorlands, and picturesque villages, such as Grosmont and Goathland.
- **Coastal Loops:**
    - Shorter loops around Whitby's harbor and West Cliff are ideal for casual riders who want a quick dose of coastal scenery. These routes often intersect with local attractions, such as Whitby Abbey and Sandsend Beach.

Horseback Riding Tours Near Whitby

Exploring Whitby's countryside on horseback provides a unique perspective and a sense of connection with the area's heritage and landscapes.

- **Local Riding Centers:**
    - **Falling Foss Riding Centre:** Situated near Whitby, this center offers guided rides tailored to different skill levels. Riders can enjoy trails that wind through woodlands, moorlands, and open fields.
    - **Borrowby Equestrian Centre:** Located within the North York Moors, this center specializes in scenic hacks that showcase the region's diverse terrain, including heather-strewn hills and winding bridleways.
- **Coastal Horse Rides:**

➢ Riding along the coastline is a bucket-list experience. Some tours include sections of the beach at low tide, offering breathtaking views of the North Sea and the dramatic cliffs.
- **Beginner-Friendly Options:**
    ➢ Many riding centers provide introductory lessons and short rides for first-timers, ensuring a safe and enjoyable experience for families and individuals new to horseback riding.

Horseback riding allows you to connect with the natural beauty of Whitby in a way that's both relaxing and invigorating.

Tips for Renting Gear and Guided Tours

To make the most of your cycling or horseback riding adventure in Whitby, preparation and local expertise are key.

- **Renting Cycling Gear:**
    ➢ **Bike Rentals:** Local businesses, such as Trailways in Hawsker, offer bike rentals for all ages and abilities. Options range from mountain bikes to e-bikes for those looking for extra support on tougher routes.
    ➢ **Safety Equipment:** Helmets and repair kits are usually included with rentals. It's advisable to check your bike's condition before setting off.
    ➢ **Route Guidance:** Many rental services provide maps and recommendations for the best trails based on your skill level and interests.
- **Booking Horse Riding Tours:**
    ➢ **Advance Reservations:** Horse riding tours are popular, especially during peak seasons. Booking in advance ensures availability and allows for customization, such as group or private rides.
    ➢ **Appropriate Attire:** Wear comfortable clothing and sturdy footwear. Riding centers typically provide helmets and other safety gear.
    ➢ **Guided Expertise:** Guides share insights about the local flora, fauna, and history, enriching the experience.

- **General Tips:**
    - **Check the Weather:** Whitby's coastal climate can be unpredictable. Dress in layers and bring waterproof gear.
    - **Respect the Environment:** Stick to designated trails and bridleways to minimize your impact on the local ecosystem.
    - **Plan for Breaks:** Carry water, snacks, and a small first-aid kit for longer journeys, whether cycling or riding.

Why Cycling and Horse Riding Are Unmissable in Whitby

Whitby's cycling paths and horse riding opportunities offer unique ways to experience the town's breathtaking scenery:

- **For Outdoor Enthusiasts:** The variety of trails ensures something for everyone, from beginner cyclists to seasoned equestrians.
- **For Families:** Safe and accessible options make these activities enjoyable for all ages.
- **For Nature Lovers:** Both cycling and horseback riding bring you closer to the region's stunning landscapes and wildlife.

Final Thoughts

Cycling and horseback riding in Whitby allow visitors to immerse themselves in the region's natural beauty and heritage. Whether pedaling along the Cinder Track or galloping across open moorlands, these activities provide unforgettable adventures that connect you to Yorkshire's landscapes. With rental services and guided tours readily available, it's easy to plan a day of exploration that suits your pace and interests. Embrace the outdoors and create lasting memories in Whitby's enchanting countryside.

Watersports and Beach Activities

Whitby's coastline is not only scenic but also a hub for water-based adventures and family-friendly beach activities. From kayaking and paddleboarding to surfing lessons and safe swimming zones, there's something for everyone along this iconic stretch of the

North Sea. This section explores the top watersports in Whitby, where to find equipment rentals and surf schools, and practical tips for enjoying the beach safely.

Kayaking and Paddleboarding Adventures

The calm waters near Whitby's harbor and along nearby coves make it an excellent destination for kayaking and paddleboarding enthusiasts.

- **Where to Kayak:**
    - **Whitby Harbor and Coastal Areas:** Launching from Whitby Harbor offers stunning views of the town's historic landmarks, including Whitby Abbey and the Whalebone Arch, from the unique perspective of the water.
    - **Saltwick Bay:** A short distance from Whitby, this bay is a favorite for kayakers seeking to explore dramatic rock formations and hidden coves.
    - **Runswick Bay:** Just north of Whitby, this peaceful bay offers a serene paddling experience with clear waters and abundant wildlife.
- **Paddleboarding Opportunities:** Paddleboarding has grown in popularity in recent years, offering a fun and accessible way to explore the coastline. Beginners can start with flat water around the harbor before venturing to slightly more open waters.
- **Guided Tours and Rentals:** Local companies offer guided tours for kayaking and paddleboarding, ensuring a safe and enjoyable experience while highlighting interesting geological features and marine life. Equipment rentals are available for those who prefer a self-guided adventure.

Surf Schools and Equipment Rentals

For those seeking an adrenaline rush, surfing is a popular activity along Whitby's coastline, with options for beginners and experienced surfers alike.

- **Best Spots for Surfing:**
    - **Cayton Bay:** Known as a surfer's paradise, this beach features consistent waves that are ideal for both novices and seasoned surfers. It's a short drive from Whitby and well worth the trip.

- **Sandsend Beach:** Closer to Whitby, Sandsend provides a quieter surfing experience with gentler waves, making it perfect for beginners.
- **Surf Schools:**
  - **Scarborough Surf School:** Located a short distance from Whitby, this school offers lessons for all ages and abilities, from introductory sessions to advanced coaching.
  - **Whitby Surf School (seasonal):** During peak months, pop-up surf schools operate near Sandsend, providing group lessons and private instruction.
- **Equipment Rentals:**
  - Surfboards, wetsuits, and bodyboards can be rented from surf shops in Whitby or directly from surf schools. Renting ensures you have high-quality, properly fitted gear for your adventure.
- **Seasonal Considerations:**
  - Summer offers warmer waters and smaller waves, ideal for beginners. Autumn and winter bring larger swells, drawing more experienced surfers.

Swimming and Safety Tips for Families

Swimming is a favorite activity for families visiting Whitby's beaches, with designated safe zones and lifeguard patrols ensuring a secure environment.

- **Best Beaches for Swimming:**
  - **Whitby Beach:** The main beach offers a safe swimming zone during the summer months, marked by flags and monitored by lifeguards. Its shallow waters are perfect for children to paddle and play.
  - **Sandsend Beach:** A quieter alternative, Sandsend also has lifeguard coverage in the peak season, providing peace of mind for families.
- **Tidal Awareness:** Whitby's beaches experience significant tidal variations. It's important to check tide times before heading out, especially for activities like swimming and rock pooling. Low tide reveals more of the sandy beach, ideal for families with young children.

- **Safety Tips for Families:**
  - ➢ **Stay in Designated Zones:** Swim only in areas monitored by lifeguards and within marked flags to avoid strong currents.
  - ➢ **Use Sunscreen:** Even on overcast days, UV rays can be strong along the coast. Apply sunscreen regularly.
  - ➢ **Bring Essentials:** Pack towels, snacks, and water for a comfortable day at the beach, and consider wetsuits for longer periods in the chilly North Sea.
  - ➢ **Supervise Children:** Always keep an eye on younger swimmers, especially during busy times or in deeper waters.

Whitby's beaches are well-equipped with amenities, including nearby cafés, restrooms, and parking, ensuring a stress-free experience for families.

Why Watersports and Beach Activities Are Unmissable in Whitby

Whitby's coastline offers an array of activities that cater to all interests and skill levels:

- **For Adventurers:** Kayaking, paddleboarding, and surfing provide thrilling ways to explore the North Sea.
- **For Families:** Safe swimming zones and child-friendly beaches ensure fun for all ages.
- **For Nature Lovers:** The opportunity to experience Whitby's dramatic coastal landscapes from the water adds a unique perspective to your visit.

Final Thoughts

Watersports and beach activities in Whitby are a must for any outdoor enthusiast or family visiting the area. Whether gliding through the harbor on a paddleboard, catching your first wave on a surfboard, or enjoying a refreshing swim in a lifeguarded zone, the coastal adventures promise memories that will last a lifetime. Embrace the thrill of the sea and the beauty of Whitby's beaches for an unforgettable seaside experience.

Chapter 8
Festivals and Events

Whitby Folk Week

Whitby Folk Week is a vibrant celebration of traditional music, dance, and storytelling that transforms this picturesque coastal town into a cultural hub every August. Drawing performers and visitors from around the UK and beyond, the festival offers a rich mix of performances, workshops, and family-friendly activities. This section explores the highlights of Whitby Folk Week, including its traditional music and dance, interactive events, and engaging experiences for families.

Traditional Music and Dance Performances

Music and dance are at the heart of Whitby Folk Week, with an impressive lineup of talented performers and ensembles showcasing the diversity of folk traditions.

- **Live Music:**
  - Throughout the week, venues across Whitby host concerts featuring renowned folk artists alongside up-and-coming talent. Expect a range of styles, from heartfelt ballads and sea shanties to lively fiddle tunes and modern interpretations of folk music.
  - Outdoor performances often take place in public spaces like the harborside or Pannett Park, adding to the festival's lively atmosphere.
- **Dance Performances:**
  - **Morris Dancing:** Teams from around the country perform colorful and energetic Morris dances, complete with bells, sticks, and traditional costumes. These displays often draw large crowds on Whitby's streets and promenades.
  - **Clog Dancing:** A nod to the region's industrial heritage, clog dancing is another popular feature of the festival, showcasing intricate footwork and rhythmic precision.

- ➢ **Social Dances:** Evening ceilidhs (traditional social dances) bring people together in a joyful celebration of music and movement. Accompanied by live bands, callers guide participants through steps, making these events accessible even to beginners.
- **Collaborative Sessions:**
  - ➢ Many festival venues host informal music sessions where musicians and singers can join in and share their talents. These gatherings provide a welcoming space for collaboration and spontaneity.

Whitby Folk Week's dedication to preserving and promoting traditional music and dance creates a dynamic and immersive experience for visitors.

Workshops and Interactive Events for Visitors

Whitby Folk Week isn't just about watching performances—it's also an opportunity to learn and participate. The festival offers a wide array of workshops and interactive events designed to engage attendees of all ages and skill levels.

- **Music Workshops:**
  - ➢ Learn to play traditional instruments like the fiddle, concertina, or tin whistle in small-group sessions led by experienced musicians.
  - ➢ Singing workshops focus on folk harmonies, storytelling through song, and shanties, allowing participants to connect with the rich oral traditions of the genre.
- **Dance Classes:**
  - ➢ Step into the world of traditional dance by joining workshops on Morris dancing, English country dancing, or even clog dancing. These classes are accessible to beginners and provide an active and fun way to immerse yourself in folk culture.
- **Storytelling and Crafts:**
  - ➢ Storytelling sessions delve into local myths, legends, and folklore, bringing the traditions of Whitby and Yorkshire to life.

- ➢ Craft workshops often focus on folk art, offering hands-on activities like weaving, pottery, or making traditional musical instruments.
- **Open Mic and Talent Shows:**
  - ➢ For those eager to share their own skills, open mic nights and talent showcases provide a supportive platform for amateur performers.

Whitby Folk Week's workshops foster a sense of community, making it a truly participatory festival where everyone can learn and create.

Family-Friendly Highlights of the Festival

Whitby Folk Week prides itself on being a family-friendly event, offering a variety of activities that cater to children and families.

- **Children's Workshops:**
  - ➢ Special workshops introduce kids to the world of folk music and dance, teaching them simple songs, rhythms, and dance steps in an engaging and fun way.
  - ➢ Instrument-making sessions let children create their own simple instruments, such as tambourines or drums, which they can then use in performances.
- **Family Ceilidhs:**
  - ➢ These lively social dances are tailored to families, with easy-to-follow instructions and energetic music that encourages everyone to join in. Family ceilidhs are a highlight for many, fostering joy and connection among participants.
- **Outdoor Performances:**
  - ➢ Whitby's open spaces host street performances, puppet shows, and interactive storytelling sessions that captivate children while introducing them to folk traditions.

- **Treasure Hunts and Trails:**
    - Activities like folklore-themed treasure hunts or trails through Whitby's historic sites engage children while showcasing the town's cultural and historical richness.

By offering engaging and accessible activities, Whitby Folk Week ensures that families leave with cherished memories.

Why Whitby Folk Week Is a Must-Attend Event

Whitby Folk Week captures the essence of traditional folk culture, making it a standout festival for music lovers, dancers, and families alike:

- **For Music Enthusiasts:** The high-quality performances and collaborative sessions provide an authentic connection to folk traditions.
- **For Learners:** Workshops and interactive events allow attendees to deepen their appreciation and understanding of folk culture.
- **For Families:** With activities designed to engage and entertain all ages, the festival fosters a welcoming and inclusive atmosphere.

Final Thoughts

Whitby Folk Week is a vibrant celebration of tradition, creativity, and community spirit. Whether you're enjoying a Morris dance performance on the cobbled streets, learning a new instrument in a workshop, or sharing a joyful ceilidh with your family, the festival offers countless ways to connect with folk culture. Set against the stunning backdrop of Whitby's harbor and historic landmarks, this annual event is a must-visit for anyone looking to experience the timeless charm of traditional music and dance.

Regatta and Maritime Events

Whitby's rich maritime heritage comes to life during its annual regatta and other nautical celebrations. These events blend competitive spirit, historical reenactments, and dazzling spectacles, creating unforgettable experiences for visitors. The **Whitby**

Regatta stands out as a highlight of the summer, offering boat races, parades, and evening fireworks that attract crowds from across the UK. This section explores the regatta's events, historical displays, and celebratory finales.

Whitby Regatta: A Mix of Races, Competitions, and Celebrations

The **Whitby Regatta**, one of the town's most anticipated events, has been a tradition for over 180 years. Taking place over a long weekend in August, it combines sportsmanship, community spirit, and entertainment.

- **Rowing and Sailing Races:**
    - The regatta's centerpiece is its series of rowing and sailing competitions, which showcase the skills of local teams and clubs.
    - **Rowing Races:** Traditional rowing skiffs, often representing Whitby and neighboring towns, compete in intense races along the harbor and coastline.
    - **Sailing Competitions:** Sailing boats of various sizes participate in races that test their crews' abilities to navigate the North Sea's challenging conditions.
- **Land-Based Competitions:**
    - Beyond the water, the regatta features quirky competitions, such as the sandcastle-building contest on Whitby Beach, drawing participants of all ages.
    - Other events include a fun run and the much-loved greasy pole contest, a test of balance and daring over the harbor waters.
- **Entertainment for All Ages:**
    - The regatta boasts fairground rides, live music performances, and street food vendors, creating a festive atmosphere that extends beyond the competitive events.
    - Families can enjoy face painting, storytelling sessions, and children's games, ensuring a day full of fun for everyone.

The regatta's combination of athleticism and entertainment makes it a cornerstone of Whitby's summer festivities.

Nautical Displays and Historical Reenactments

Whitby's maritime history takes center stage during the regatta, with displays and activities that pay homage to its seafaring past.

- **Nautical Displays:**
    - Visitors can explore ships moored in the harbor, including historical vessels and working fishing boats. Guided tours provide insights into the lives of sailors, fishermen, and shipbuilders who have shaped Whitby's identity.
    - Exhibits showcase maritime artifacts, from navigation tools to model ships, connecting visitors with the town's proud nautical heritage.
- **Historical Reenactments:**
    - Costumed performers recreate scenes from Whitby's maritime history, such as life aboard a 19th-century whaling ship or Captain Cook's early voyages.
    - Mock battles and demonstrations of old-fashioned sailing techniques captivate audiences while educating them about Whitby's role in maritime exploration.
- **Lifeboat Demonstrations:**
    - The Royal National Lifeboat Institution (RNLI) hosts live demonstrations, highlighting the bravery and expertise of lifeboat crews. Visitors gain a new appreciation for the vital role these crews play in safeguarding lives at sea.

The nautical displays and reenactments create a deeper connection to Whitby's storied maritime traditions, enriching the regatta experience.

Evening Fireworks and Parades

The regatta culminates in a series of evening celebrations that light up the town, leaving visitors with lasting memories.

- **Grand Parade:**
  - The **regatta parade** winds through Whitby's streets, featuring floats, marching bands, and costumed performers. Locals and visitors alike line the streets to cheer on participants and revel in the lively atmosphere.
  - The parade often incorporates themes that reflect Whitby's culture and history, with creative decorations and community involvement adding to the spectacle.
- **Fireworks Display:**
  - A dazzling fireworks show over the harbor marks the grand finale of the regatta. The vibrant colors illuminate Whitby's iconic landmarks, including the Abbey and West Cliff, creating a breathtaking scene.
  - Accompanied by music, the display offers a fitting end to a weekend of festivities, leaving visitors with unforgettable images of Whitby's beauty and energy.
- **Evening Entertainment:**
  - Local pubs, restaurants, and event spaces host live music and performances throughout the evening, ensuring that the celebration continues long after the fireworks have faded.

The evening events bring the community together in a spirit of celebration, showcasing the best of Whitby's hospitality and charm.

Why Whitby Regatta and Maritime Events Are Unmissable

The Whitby Regatta and associated maritime events provide a unique blend of history, competition, and celebration:

- **For Sports Enthusiasts:** The thrilling boat races and competitions highlight the skill and determination of local athletes.

- **For History Buffs:** Nautical displays and reenactments offer a fascinating glimpse into Whitby's maritime legacy.
- **For Families:** The regatta's entertainment and activities ensure a memorable experience for visitors of all ages.

Final Thoughts

The Whitby Regatta is a highlight of the town's calendar, combining thrilling races, immersive history, and vibrant celebrations. Whether cheering on rowers, exploring historical ships, or marveling at the evening fireworks, visitors are sure to be captivated by the energy and charm of this cherished event. Whitby's maritime traditions come alive during the regatta, making it a must-see for anyone visiting this iconic coastal town.

Christmas in Whitby

Whitby transforms into a winter wonderland during the holiday season, offering visitors a magical mix of festive markets, dazzling decorations, and cheerful events. From Christmas markets filled with local crafts to ice skating and enchanting New Year's Eve celebrations by the harbor, Whitby provides a warm and welcoming atmosphere that captures the spirit of the season. This section highlights the key attractions of a Whitby Christmas, showcasing why the town is a must-visit destination during the holidays.

Festive Markets and Decorations

Whitby's festive markets and holiday decorations bring the town's charm to life, creating a delightful setting for seasonal shopping and exploration.

- **Whitby Christmas Market:**
    - Held in the heart of town, the Christmas market is a hub of activity, featuring stalls brimming with handmade gifts, artisanal foods, and holiday treats.

- Local vendors showcase unique items like Whitby jet jewelry, handcrafted ornaments, and gourmet preserves, making it an ideal place to find one-of-a-kind presents.
  - Live music and performances add to the festive atmosphere, with carolers and brass bands spreading holiday cheer.
- **Decorations and Lighting:**
  - Whitby's streets are adorned with twinkling lights and festive decorations, enhancing the town's magical ambiance. The harbor glows with illuminated boats, and shop windows compete with creative holiday displays.
  - The Christmas tree at Dock End serves as a central focal point, providing a perfect spot for photos and gatherings.
- **Seasonal Food and Drink:**
  - Stalls and nearby cafés offer mulled wine, roasted chestnuts, and mince pies, inviting visitors to indulge in traditional holiday flavors while browsing the market.

The combination of vibrant markets and enchanting decorations makes Whitby a captivating holiday destination for visitors of all ages.

Ice Skating and Seasonal Events

Whitby's holiday festivities extend beyond shopping to include family-friendly events and winter activities that add to the season's joy.

- **Ice Skating:**
  - A pop-up ice rink in Pannett Park or near the harbor often becomes a highlight of Whitby's Christmas season. Families and couples alike enjoy gliding across the ice, surrounded by the town's festive lights.
  - Skating sessions are typically paired with music and hot refreshments, creating a magical experience for participants.

- **Santa's Grotto:**
  - Children can meet Santa Claus at various locations around town, including festive markets and local attractions. These visits often include photo opportunities and small gifts, ensuring a memorable experience for little ones.
- **Caroling and Performances:**
  - Whitby hosts caroling events in its historic churches, such as St. Mary's Church, and around the harbor. These gatherings create a sense of community and tradition, with classic Christmas songs filling the air.
  - Local theaters and venues, like the Whitby Pavilion, present seasonal performances, including pantomimes, concerts, and festive plays.

These events ensure that the holiday spirit is alive and thriving in Whitby, offering something for everyone to enjoy.

New Year's Eve Celebrations Along the Harbor

Whitby's New Year's Eve festivities provide the perfect way to ring in the new year, with celebrations that blend tradition and excitement.

- **Harbor Fireworks:**
  - The highlight of Whitby's New Year's Eve is the spectacular fireworks display over the harbor. As the clock strikes midnight, the skies light up with dazzling colors, reflecting beautifully on the water.
  - Crowds gather along the harbor and West Cliff to watch the display, creating a communal atmosphere of celebration and joy.
- **Pub Celebrations and Live Music:**
  - Whitby's historic pubs, such as The Duke of York and The Black Horse Inn, host lively New Year's Eve parties featuring live music, dancing, and a festive menu.
  - Many establishments organize countdowns and themed events, ensuring a night of fun and entertainment for all.

- **Harbor Processions and Midnight Gatherings:**
    - In addition to fireworks, some years feature processions or community gatherings at Dock End, where locals and visitors come together to celebrate. These gatherings often include traditional Yorkshire customs, adding a cultural touch to the festivities.

Whitby's New Year's Eve celebrations provide a memorable way to welcome the coming year in a picturesque seaside setting.

Why Christmas in Whitby Is Unmissable

A holiday season in Whitby offers an enchanting mix of activities, making it a must-visit destination during winter:

- **For Families:** Santa's grotto, ice skating, and festive markets provide endless entertainment for children and adults alike.
- **For Shoppers:** Unique, handcrafted gifts at the Christmas market ensure a rewarding shopping experience.
- **For Celebrants:** The New Year's Eve fireworks and harbor celebrations create a magical start to the year.

Final Thoughts

Christmas in Whitby is a time of joy, celebration, and community spirit. From the twinkling lights of its festive markets to the excitement of New Year's Eve fireworks over the harbor, the town embraces the holiday season with warmth and charm. Whether you're skating under the stars, shopping for unique gifts, or singing carols by the sea, Whitby offers unforgettable memories and a truly magical winter experience.

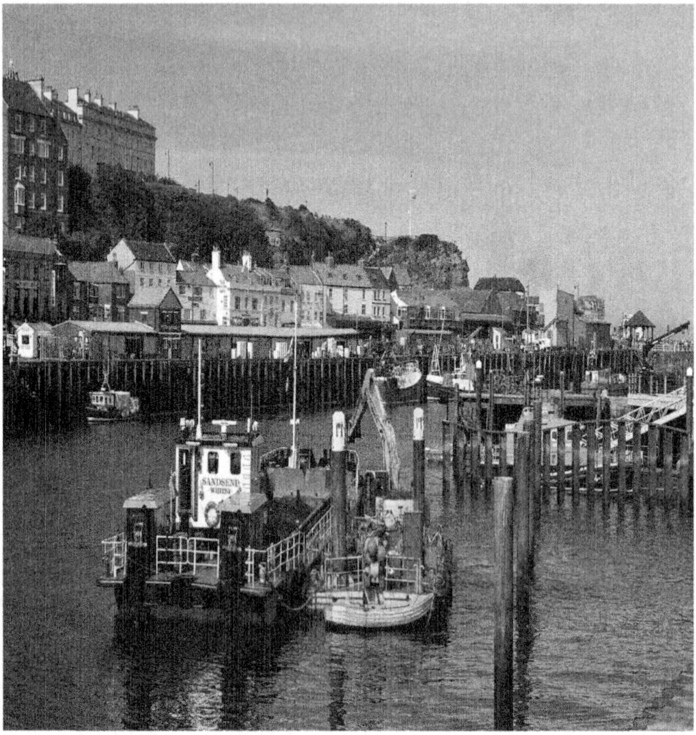

Chapter 9
Shopping and Local Crafts

Whitby Jet and Jewelry

Whitby jet is a gemstone as iconic to the town as its Abbey or coastline. This beautiful, glossy black gem, steeped in history and crafted into exquisite jewelry, has been a hallmark of Whitby for centuries. Visitors come from around the world to explore its rich legacy, shop for unique pieces, and learn to distinguish authentic jet from imitations. This section delves into the history of Whitby jet, the artisans and studios that craft it, and practical tips for identifying genuine jet jewelry.

History of Whitby Jet Mining and Craftsmanship

Whitby jet is a type of fossilized wood, originating from the **Araucaria tree**, which grew in the region over 180 million years ago during the Jurassic period.

- **Formation and Characteristics:**
  - Over millions of years, wood from these trees was buried and compressed under sediment, undergoing a natural fossilization process. The result is a dense, lightweight material with a deep black sheen.
- **Historical Significance:**
  - **Roman Times:** The use of Whitby jet dates back to Roman Britain when it was crafted into beads and amulets believed to ward off evil spirits.
  - **Victorian Era Popularity:** Jet reached its peak during the Victorian era when Queen Victoria adopted it as mourning jewelry following the death of Prince Albert. Its somber elegance made it the material of choice for brooches, necklaces, and earrings.
  - **Modern Appeal:** Today, Whitby jet remains a sought-after material, prized for its beauty and historical significance.

- **Mining in Whitby:**
    - Historically, jet was collected from cliffs and beaches around Whitby, often during low tide. By the 19th century, small-scale mining operations emerged to meet demand.
    - Jet mining has since ceased due to environmental concerns, but artisans continue to work with existing supplies of the gemstone, ensuring its legacy endures.

Whitby jet's rich history intertwines with the cultural and economic story of the town, making it a must-learn topic for visitors.

Shops and Studios Specializing in Jet Jewelry

Whitby is home to an array of shops and studios where skilled artisans create stunning pieces of jet jewelry. These establishments offer a unique shopping experience, allowing visitors to witness craftsmanship firsthand.

- **Top Jet Jewelry Shops:**
    - **W Hamond:** Known as "The Original Whitby Jet Shop," W Hamond has been crafting jet jewelry since 1860. Their collection features everything from classic Victorian designs to contemporary pieces, often combined with silver or gold.
    - **The Ebor Jet Works:** This boutique offers handcrafted jet jewelry and provides detailed insights into the history and craftsmanship behind each piece.
    - **Whitby Jet Heritage Centre:** Both a workshop and a retail space, this establishment allows visitors to observe artisans at work while exploring the processes behind creating intricate jet designs.
- **Workshops and Custom Creations:** Many studios offer bespoke services, allowing customers to design unique pieces tailored to their preferences. Visitors can choose settings, additional gemstones, and styles, creating a truly one-of-a-kind keepsake.

- **Variety of Designs:**
    - Traditional Victorian mourning designs remain popular, but contemporary creations now dominate the market, featuring sleek, modern aesthetics.
    - Jet is often paired with materials like sterling silver, pearls, or even vibrant gemstones to create striking contrasts.

These shops and studios celebrate the artistry and heritage of Whitby jet, ensuring its timeless appeal for generations to come.

How to Identify Authentic Whitby Jet

Given the popularity of Whitby jet, imitations are common, making it essential for buyers to know how to distinguish genuine jet from counterfeit materials.

- **Physical Characteristics:**
    - **Lightweight:** Authentic Whitby jet is surprisingly light, making it comfortable to wear in large pieces.
    - **Warm to the Touch:** Unlike synthetic substitutes or glass, jet feels warm when held in your hand due to its organic nature.
    - **Deep Black Color:** Genuine jet has a rich, velvety black appearance that is unmatched by imitations.
- **Simple Tests:**
    - **The Streak Test:** When rubbed against unglazed porcelain, authentic jet leaves a brown streak, while imitations may leave black or other colors.
    - **The Scratch Test:** Jet is softer than many counterfeit materials and can be gently scratched with a pin. However, this test should only be done on unpolished pieces or scraps.
- **Certifications and Trustworthy Sellers:**
    - Reputable Whitby jet retailers often provide certificates of authenticity, guaranteeing the material's origin.

> Shopping from established stores like W Hamond or The Whitby Jet Heritage Centre ensures you are purchasing genuine jet, crafted by skilled artisans.

- **Avoiding Common Imitations:**
    > Look out for substitutes like black glass, resin, or plastic, which may mimic jet's appearance but lack its depth and warmth.

Knowing these tips helps buyers appreciate the value and craftsmanship of Whitby jet while ensuring their investment in an authentic piece.

Why Whitby Jet Jewelry Is a Must-Buy Souvenir

Whitby jet jewelry is more than just an accessory—it's a piece of history and a testament to the town's artisanal excellence:

- **For History Enthusiasts:** Jet connects you to Whitby's Roman roots and Victorian traditions.
- **For Fashion Lovers:** The timeless elegance of jet jewelry suits both classic and contemporary styles.
- **For Artisanship Appreciators:** Each piece reflects the skill and dedication of Whitby's craftsmen.

Final Thoughts

Whitby jet jewelry is a quintessential part of the town's identity, offering visitors a chance to own a beautiful, meaningful piece of its heritage. From the gemstone's ancient origins to its transformation into exquisite works of art, Whitby jet embodies history, artistry, and timeless elegance. Exploring the town's jet shops and studios, learning about its craftsmanship, and selecting an authentic piece make for a memorable and enriching experience.

Artisan Markets and Boutiques

Whitby is a treasure trove of creativity and craftsmanship, offering a delightful shopping experience that highlights the talents of local artisans. From handmade souvenirs and unique gifts to fresh produce and baked goods at farmers' markets, the town's markets and boutiques capture its charm and heritage. This section delves into Whitby's artisan scene, spotlighting local crafts, farmers' markets, and independent shops for distinctive finds.

Local Crafts and Handmade Souvenirs

Whitby's artisan markets and craft shops celebrate the town's creativity, with vendors offering unique, handmade items that make perfect keepsakes or gifts.

- **Traditional Crafts:**
  - Many artisans in Whitby draw inspiration from the town's maritime heritage and natural surroundings, crafting items like driftwood sculptures, hand-carved wooden ornaments, and nautical-themed pottery.
  - Whitby's famous **jet** also appears in locally made accessories, such as jet-embellished trinket boxes and keychains, offering a more affordable alternative to jewelry.
- **Handmade Textiles and Clothing:**
  - Local artisans craft cozy knitwear, scarves, and socks, often made with Yorkshire wool, ensuring both quality and a connection to the region's textile traditions.
  - Shoppers can find custom designs at workshops specializing in screen-printed T-shirts, tote bags, and aprons featuring Whitby-inspired imagery.
- **Artisan Markets:**
  - Seasonal craft fairs and pop-up markets are common throughout the year, showcasing items such as candles, soaps, and bespoke home décor. These markets are ideal for discovering one-of-a-kind treasures and supporting small businesses.

Handmade crafts in Whitby reflect the town's character, blending traditional techniques with modern creativity to create meaningful souvenirs.

Farmers' Markets with Fresh Produce and Baked Goods

Farmers' markets in Whitby offer more than just shopping—they're a celebration of the region's agricultural bounty and culinary traditions.

- **Fresh Produce:**
  - Local farmers bring fresh fruits, vegetables, and herbs straight from their fields to market stalls. Seasonal offerings like strawberries, apples, and rhubarb reflect the region's changing seasons.
  - Shoppers can also find locally produced honey, jams, and chutneys, often made with traditional recipes that highlight the area's flavors.
- **Baked Goods and Treats:**
  - Bakers at Whitby's farmers' markets present a tempting array of breads, pastries, and cakes. Specialties include Yorkshire curd tarts, scones, and parkin—a ginger-spiced cake that's a local favorite.
  - For those with a sweet tooth, fudge and chocolate stalls provide irresistible options, many incorporating local ingredients like Whitby's famous sea salt.
- **Popular Markets:**
  - **Whitby Farmers' Market:** Held monthly in the town center, this market is a hub for fresh produce and artisanal goods. It's an excellent place to sample local flavors and meet the producers behind them.
  - **Nearby Markets:** Visitors willing to venture slightly farther afield can explore markets in Scarborough and Pickering, offering even more variety.

Farmers' markets not only provide delicious, high-quality goods but also offer a chance to connect with the community and learn about Whitby's culinary heritage.

Unique Gifts from Whitby's Independent Boutiques

Whitby's independent boutiques are brimming with personality and creativity, making them perfect destinations for discovering distinctive gifts and treasures.

- **Bookshops and Stationery:**
    - Independent bookshops in Whitby stock an eclectic mix of titles, from local history and maritime tales to gothic novels inspired by *Dracula*.
    - Boutique stationery stores offer handcrafted journals, greeting cards, and prints, often featuring Whitby landmarks or coastal scenes.
- **Art Galleries and Studios:**
    - Galleries like the Whitby Galleries showcase paintings, prints, and sculptures created by local artists. Popular themes include dramatic seascapes, harbor scenes, and Whitby Abbey, capturing the essence of the town.
    - Many studios sell prints, postcards, and miniature reproductions of their work, providing affordable ways to bring home a piece of Whitby's artistic spirit.
- **Home Décor and Gifts:**
    - Shops specializing in coastal and nautical décor offer everything from hand-painted ceramics and driftwood mirrors to sea-themed cushions and wall art.
    - Whitby-themed gifts like mugs, magnets, and tea towels featuring the town's landmarks are popular keepsakes for visitors.
- **Eco-Friendly and Sustainable Options:**
    - Several boutiques focus on sustainability, selling items like reusable bags, bamboo utensils, and locally made natural skincare products. These shops align with modern eco-conscious values while offering unique, practical souvenirs.

The variety and quality of goods in Whitby's independent boutiques ensure there's something for every taste and interest.

Why Artisan Markets and Boutiques Are a Must-Visit

Whitby's artisan markets and boutiques offer more than just shopping—they're an opportunity to connect with the town's culture and creativity:

- **For Craft Lovers:** Handmade souvenirs and unique gifts showcase the talent of local artisans.
- **For Foodies:** Farmers' markets provide a chance to sample and bring home the best of Yorkshire's culinary offerings.
- **For Art Enthusiasts:** Independent boutiques and galleries offer stunning pieces that capture the beauty and spirit of Whitby.

Final Thoughts

Whitby's artisan markets and boutiques are a testament to the town's vibrant creative scene. From browsing handcrafted treasures and sampling freshly baked treats to discovering unique gifts in charming shops, every shopping experience is infused with the character of this coastal gem. Visitors leave not only with memorable finds but also with a deeper appreciation for the artistry and community spirit that make Whitby truly special.

Antiques and Vintage Finds

Whitby is a haven for treasure hunters, offering a wealth of antique shops and vintage stores filled with unique pieces that reflect the town's rich history and charm. From discovering timeless collectibles to browsing retro fashion, shopping for antiques in Whitby is an adventure in itself. This section explores the town's best antique stores, the allure of vintage fashion, and tips for uncovering hidden gems.

Treasure Hunting in Whitby's Antique Shops

Whitby's antique shops are brimming with character, offering a range of treasures that tell stories of the past.

- **Antique Furniture and Home Décor:**
    - Many of Whitby's antique shops feature furniture and home items from different eras, including Victorian pieces, maritime-inspired décor, and unique trinkets. These items make perfect souvenirs or statement pieces for your home.
    - **The Whitby Antiques Centre:** Located in the town center, this multi-dealer space showcases a variety of antiques, including jewelry, glassware, and furniture, ensuring a diverse shopping experience.
- **Maritime Collectibles:**
    - As a historic coastal town, Whitby boasts a selection of maritime-themed antiques, such as ship models, compasses, and sailor's keepsakes. These pieces highlight Whitby's connection to the sea and its seafaring traditions.
- **Historical Memorabilia:**
    - Many shops feature items tied to Whitby's history, including Victorian photographs, old postcards, and memorabilia linked to Captain Cook or *Dracula*.

Exploring Whitby's antique stores offers a unique opportunity to uncover one-of-a-kind finds that reflect the town's rich heritage and artistic legacy.

Vintage Fashion and Collectibles

Vintage enthusiasts will find plenty to love in Whitby, from retro clothing to collectible items that evoke the glamour of bygone eras.

- **Clothing and Accessories:**
    - Whitby's vintage boutiques and markets offer a range of carefully curated pieces, including flapper dresses, leather jackets, and accessories like brooches, scarves, and handbags.
    - Many shops specialize in styles from the 1920s through the 1980s, ensuring a diverse selection to suit various tastes.

- **Whitby's Gothic Influence:**
  - Given the town's connection to Gothic culture, vintage stores often feature darker, dramatic pieces that align with the aesthetic. Look for flowing capes, Victorian-inspired blouses, and statement jewelry.
- **Collectibles and Curiosities:**
  - Whitby's shops often feature quirky collectibles, such as vintage toys, rare books, and vinyl records. These items make excellent gifts or conversation starters.
  - For fans of *Dracula* or gothic literature, some stores stock first-edition books, themed memorabilia, and artwork that pays homage to Whitby's literary connections.
- **Notable Stores:**
  - **Dotty About Vintage:** This boutique is known for its handpicked selection of clothing and accessories, offering both quality and character.
  - **The Emporium:** A treasure trove of vintage and antique items, including jewelry, homeware, and collectibles.

Shopping for vintage fashion and collectibles in Whitby combines style with nostalgia, making it a rewarding experience for visitors.

Tips for Finding Hidden Gems

Antique and vintage shopping is an art, and knowing how to hunt effectively can help you uncover remarkable pieces in Whitby's shops and markets.

- **Be Patient and Explore Thoroughly:**
  - Antiques and vintage items often require time to sift through, so be prepared to browse methodically. Hidden gems are frequently tucked away in corners or overlooked sections of the store.
- **Ask Questions:**
  - Shop owners and dealers are often passionate about their collections and can provide valuable insights into an item's history, authenticity, or use. Don't hesitate to ask about the story behind a piece.

- **Look for Quality:**
    - Examine items carefully for signs of damage or wear. While minor imperfections can add character, ensure the piece is structurally sound, especially for furniture or jewelry.
- **Know What You're Looking For:**
    - While it's fun to browse, having a general idea of what you're interested in—whether it's mid-century décor, vintage clothing, or maritime memorabilia—can make your search more focused.
- **Haggle Politely:**
    - Many antique dealers are open to negotiation, especially for higher-value items or multiple purchases. Approach haggling respectfully, and you may secure a better price.
- **Visit During Quiet Times:**
    - Shopping on weekdays or early in the day often provides a more relaxed experience, allowing you to browse without crowds and have more in-depth conversations with sellers.

By following these tips, you can maximize your chances of finding exceptional items and making your antique shopping experience in Whitby truly rewarding.

Why Antiques and Vintage Finds Are a Must-Explore in Whitby

Whitby's antique and vintage stores are more than just shops—they're portals to the past:

- **For History Buffs:** Discover treasures that reflect Whitby's maritime heritage and Victorian charm.
- **For Collectors:** Find rare, one-of-a-kind pieces to add to your collection.
- **For Style Seekers:** Embrace vintage fashion and décor that stands out with timeless appeal.

Final Thoughts

Whitby's antique and vintage shopping scene is a delightful mix of history, craftsmanship, and nostalgia. From unique collectibles in charming boutiques to maritime-themed antiques and retro clothing, each item tells a story and offers a glimpse into the past. Whether you're an avid collector or a casual shopper, Whitby's shops provide the perfect opportunity to find something truly special while immersing yourself in the town's rich heritage.

Chapter 10
Practical Tips for Visitors

Budget Travel Tips

Visiting Whitby on a budget doesn't mean compromising on experience. The town offers a range of affordable accommodations, dining options, and free activities that allow visitors to immerse themselves in its charm without overspending. By taking advantage of seasonal discounts and travel passes, visitors can enjoy a fulfilling trip while keeping costs in check. This section highlights how to explore Whitby affordably, covering lodging, dining, attractions, and money-saving strategies.

Affordable Accommodations and Dining Options

Whitby caters to all budgets with its variety of accommodations and eateries, offering comfort and quality without breaking the bank.

- **Budget-Friendly Accommodations:**
  - **Guesthouses and B&Bs:** Many family-run bed-and-breakfasts in Whitby provide cozy stays at reasonable rates, especially if booked well in advance. Options like **The Riviera Guesthouse** and **The Sanders Yard** offer excellent value, with hearty breakfasts included.
  - **Hostels:** For budget-conscious travelers or solo adventurers, hostels like **YHA Whitby** provide clean, comfortable rooms and shared facilities at minimal cost. Its location near Whitby Abbey adds extra appeal.
  - **Vacation Rentals:** Renting an apartment or cottage can be a cost-effective option for families or groups, allowing you to save on meals by cooking your own food. Websites like Airbnb or local letting agencies offer numerous choices.
  - **Off-Peak Discounts:** Prices for accommodations tend to drop during off-peak seasons, such as autumn and winter (excluding holidays). Booking midweek rather than weekends can also reduce costs.

- **Dining on a Budget:**
    - ➢ **Traditional Fish and Chips:** Whitby is famous for its fish and chips, and affordable spots like **Trenchers** or **Hadley's Fish Restaurant** offer delicious portions that won't strain your wallet.
    - ➢ **Cafés and Bakeries:** Local cafés such as **Botham's of Whitby** serve inexpensive sandwiches, pastries, and Yorkshire specialties like parkin, perfect for a light lunch.
    - ➢ **Pubs:** Many pubs, like **The Duke of York**, offer budget-friendly meals, including hearty pies, burgers, and Sunday roasts.
    - ➢ **Picnics:** For an even cheaper option, shop for fresh produce, bread, and local cheese at **Whitby Farmers' Market**, and enjoy a picnic at scenic spots like Pannett Park or along the harbor.

Free Attractions and Activities

Whitby offers a wealth of free or low-cost attractions that highlight its natural beauty and cultural heritage.

- **Explore Whitby's Beaches:**
    - ➢ Stroll along **Whitby Beach** or venture to quieter spots like **Sandsend Beach**. Enjoy activities such as rock pooling, fossil hunting, or simply relaxing by the sea—completely free of charge.
- **The 199 Steps and St. Mary's Church:**
    - ➢ Climb the **199 Steps** for panoramic views of Whitby Harbor and coastline. At the top, visit the historic **St. Mary's Church** and its atmospheric graveyard, which inspired *Dracula*.
- **Whitby Abbey Grounds:**
    - ➢ While entry to Whitby Abbey requires a ticket, you can explore the surrounding grounds and enjoy breathtaking views of the Abbey ruins and the North Sea without a fee.

- **Whitby Harbour and West Pier:**
  - Wander along the harbor and West Pier to take in the bustling maritime activity and stunning sea views. Bring a camera for snapshots of the iconic **Whalebone Arch** and the lighthouse.
- **Pannett Park:**
  - This beautifully maintained park in the town center offers peaceful walking paths, vibrant flower gardens, and free family-friendly fun.
- **Cultural Events:**
  - Keep an eye out for free performances and events during festivals like **Whitby Folk Week** or the **Whitby Regatta**, which often include open-air concerts and parades.

Whitby's free attractions ensure that visitors can experience the town's highlights without spending a penny.

Seasonal Discounts and Travel Passes

Smart planning and taking advantage of seasonal deals can significantly reduce travel expenses.

- **Seasonal Discounts:**
  - **Off-Peak Deals:** Many accommodations and attractions offer discounted rates during quieter times of the year, such as January through March or November (outside of holiday periods).
  - **Festival Offers:** During events like the **Whitby Goth Weekend**, some local businesses provide special promotions on food, drinks, or souvenirs.
  - **Last-Minute Deals:** Check local tourism websites or booking platforms for last-minute discounts on accommodations or activities.
- **Travel Passes:**
  - **Whitby and North Yorkshire Moors Travel Pass:** For visitors planning to explore beyond Whitby, this pass offers discounts on public transportation and some local attractions in the surrounding area.

- ➢ **English Heritage Membership:** If you're visiting multiple historical sites in the region, including Whitby Abbey, consider investing in an English Heritage membership for free entry and additional perks.
- ➢ **Rail Passes:** If traveling by train, railcards like the **Two Together Railcard** or **Family and Friends Railcard** can save up to 33% on fares to Whitby.
- **Group Discounts and Family Tickets:**
  - ➢ Many attractions, including museums and boat tours, offer reduced rates for families or groups. Planning activities together can result in substantial savings.

By planning around seasonal offers and utilizing travel passes, visitors can stretch their budgets without sacrificing quality experiences.

Why Budget Travel in Whitby Is Rewarding

Whitby proves that memorable travel experiences don't have to come at a high price:

- **For Nature Lovers:** The town's beaches, parks, and harbor walks provide endless enjoyment at no cost.
- **For History Buffs:** Free landmarks like the 199 Steps and St. Mary's Church offer insight into Whitby's rich past.
- **For Savvy Shoppers:** Seasonal discounts and travel passes make Whitby accessible for all budgets.

Final Thoughts

Whitby's blend of affordable accommodations, free attractions, and budget-friendly dining makes it an excellent destination for travelers looking to experience its charm without overspending. By taking advantage of seasonal deals and embracing the town's natural and cultural offerings, visitors can enjoy a fulfilling trip that's as economical as it is memorable. From savoring fish and chips to exploring stunning beaches, Whitby invites you to discover its beauty without breaking the bank.

Accessibility and Comfort

Whitby's charming cobbled streets, historical sites, and natural beauty make it a delightful destination for visitors of all abilities. While the town's steep inclines and heritage buildings pose some challenges, many attractions and amenities cater to wheelchair users, families with young children, and those seeking a stress-free travel experience. This section highlights wheelchair-friendly routes, family amenities, and tips for navigating Whitby with ease.

Wheelchair-Friendly Routes and Attractions

Whitby has made strides in improving accessibility, offering several wheelchair-friendly routes and attractions that ensure everyone can enjoy the town's highlights.

- **Accessible Attractions:**
  - **Whitby Abbey:** While the Abbey ruins themselves involve uneven terrain, the visitor center is wheelchair-accessible, offering exhibits and breathtaking views of the coastline.
  - **Pannett Park:** This serene park features smooth, paved paths and accessible entrances, making it a relaxing spot for visitors with mobility challenges.
  - **Whitby Museum:** Located within Pannett Park, the museum provides ramp access and elevators, ensuring all visitors can explore its exhibits on Whitby's history, fossils, and maritime heritage.
  - **Whitby Harbour:** The harborside offers a flat, paved promenade that is ideal for wheelchair users and those with limited mobility, providing stunning views of boats and the bustling waterfront.
- **Wheelchair-Accessible Transportation:**
  - Whitby's **Coastliner Buses** are equipped with low floors and wheelchair spaces, allowing easy travel to nearby destinations like Robin Hood's Bay or Scarborough.
  - **Taxis:** Local taxi services often accommodate wheelchairs with advance notice, ensuring stress-free transportation around town.

- **Tips for Accessibility:**
  - Some cobbled streets, such as Church Street, can be challenging for wheelchair users. Stick to smoother routes along the harbor and newer areas of town.
  - Accessible parking is available at several locations, including Abbey Headland and near the harbor.

Whitby's accessible routes and attractions make it possible for everyone to enjoy the town's charm and history.

Family-Friendly Amenities for Travelers with Kids

Traveling with children in Whitby is made easier by its variety of family-friendly amenities and attractions tailored to young visitors.

- **Child-Friendly Attractions:**
  - **Whitby Beach:** Safe, sandy stretches and lifeguarded zones make the beach ideal for families. Kids can enjoy building sandcastles, paddling in shallow waters, or searching for fossils along the shore.
  - **Pannett Park:** The park includes a children's play area with swings, climbing frames, and picnic spots, offering a perfect space for little ones to burn off energy.
  - **Captain Cook Memorial Museum:** Interactive exhibits and family-friendly storytelling sessions make this museum engaging for children curious about Whitby's maritime history.
- **Dining with Kids:**
  - Many pubs and cafés in Whitby, such as **The Magpie Café** and **Trenchers**, offer kid-friendly menus with options like fish fingers, chips, and ice cream. High chairs and baby-changing facilities are commonly available.
- **Practical Amenities:**
  - Baby-changing facilities are located in public restrooms near the harbor and in popular attractions like the museum.

> Family rooms in hotels and guesthouses provide spacious accommodations for travelers with young children.
- **Tips for Families:**
  > Strollers may struggle on cobbled streets or steep paths, so consider bringing a baby carrier for easier mobility.
  > Plan beach visits during low tide for maximum space and safety.

Whitby's family-friendly offerings ensure that visitors of all ages have a memorable and enjoyable experience.

Tips for Stress-Free Navigation of Whitby

Whitby's layout, with its mix of steep inclines, cobbled streets, and bustling harbor, can be tricky to navigate without preparation. These tips help ensure a smooth and stress-free visit.

- **Planning Routes:**
  > Use smoother streets like Baxtergate and Flowergate for easier navigation, especially if pushing a stroller or using a wheelchair. Avoid steep areas such as the 199 Steps unless prepared for a challenge.
  > Maps highlighting accessible routes are often available from the **Tourist Information Centre**, located near the harbor.
- **Parking Options:**
  > Whitby offers several car parks, including accessible spaces at Church Street and Abbey Headland. During peak times, park-and-ride services provide convenient alternatives, reducing the stress of finding parking in town.
- **Public Transport:**
  > Trains to Whitby are generally accessible, with ramps and staff assistance available at larger stations like Scarborough or Middlesbrough. Ensure to check in advance for specific requirements.

- **Avoiding Crowds:**
    - Whitby's popularity can lead to crowds during weekends and festivals. Visiting early in the morning or midweek ensures a more relaxed experience, particularly at popular sites like the Abbey or harbor.
- **Weather Preparation:**
    - Whitby's coastal weather can be unpredictable. Dress in layers, carry waterproofs, and wear sturdy footwear for uneven surfaces.
- **Using Technology:**
    - Navigation apps can help you find accessible routes, parking, and public transport options. Look for platforms that cater specifically to travelers with mobility challenges.

These practical tips make it easier to explore Whitby's charms with minimal hassle, ensuring a pleasant experience for all visitors.

Why Accessibility and Comfort Matter in Whitby

Whitby's efforts to accommodate visitors of all abilities and needs enhance the experience for everyone:

- **For Wheelchair Users:** Smooth paths and accessible attractions ensure inclusivity.
- **For Families:** Kid-friendly amenities and attractions make Whitby an excellent choice for a family getaway.
- **For Stress-Free Travelers:** Proper planning and navigation tips make exploring Whitby enjoyable and effortless.

Final Thoughts

Whitby's charm extends to its accessibility and comfort for visitors of all ages and abilities. With wheelchair-friendly routes, family-friendly amenities, and thoughtful planning, exploring this historic seaside town becomes a delightful experience. Whether it's enjoying the harbor promenade, discovering child-friendly attractions, or navigating with ease, Whitby offers practical solutions for every traveler to make the most of their visit.

Packing and Preparation

Planning a trip to Whitby is as much about preparation as it is about anticipation. The town's coastal climate, diverse activities, and historical charm require a thoughtful packing list to ensure a comfortable and enjoyable experience. This section provides guidance on what to pack for Whitby's weather, essentials for outdoor adventures and events, and how to stay connected during your visit.

What to Pack for Whitby's Coastal Climate

Whitby's location on the North Yorkshire coast gives it a maritime climate, with mild temperatures and occasional unpredictable weather. Packing appropriately ensures you're ready for all conditions.

- **Clothing for Layering:**
  - Coastal weather can change quickly, so pack layers that can be added or removed as needed. A combination of T-shirts, sweaters, and lightweight jackets is ideal.
  - Even in summer, evenings by the sea can be chilly. Bring a warm fleece or windbreaker for extra comfort.
- **Rain Protection:**
  - Showers are frequent in Whitby, so a waterproof jacket or compact raincoat is essential.
  - Consider packing a small, travel-friendly umbrella for lighter rain.
- **Comfortable Footwear:**
  - Cobblestone streets, coastal trails, and sandy beaches call for sturdy, comfortable shoes. Walking boots or trainers are ideal for hikes, while waterproof shoes or sandals work well for beach outings.

- **Seasonal Accessories:**
    - **Summer:** Pack sunglasses, sunscreen, and a hat to protect against UV rays during long days outdoors.
    - **Winter:** Bring a scarf, gloves, and a beanie to stay warm against brisk sea breezes.
- **Backpack or Daypack:**
    - A small backpack is handy for carrying water, snacks, a camera, and extra layers during day trips or hikes.

By packing for Whitby's variable weather, you'll be prepared to enjoy its natural beauty and outdoor activities in any season.

Essentials for Hiking, Festivals, and Boat Trips

Whitby offers a variety of activities, from coastal hikes and historical festivals to scenic boat tours. Tailoring your packing list to these experiences ensures you're ready for adventure.

- **For Hiking and Coastal Walks:**
    - **Maps and Guides:** While many trails are well-marked, carrying a physical map or guidebook ensures you stay on track. Apps like AllTrails can also be helpful for navigation.
    - **Hydration and Snacks:** Pack a reusable water bottle and energy bars for longer treks like the Cleveland Way or trails to Robin Hood's Bay.
    - **Weather Protection:** A lightweight, packable rain jacket is crucial, along with a hat for sun protection.
- **For Festivals and Events:**
    - **Comfortable Clothing:** Festivals like **Whitby Folk Week** or **Whitby Goth Weekend** may involve long days of walking or standing. Wear comfortable shoes and dress in layers to adjust to changing temperatures.
    - **Themed Accessories:** Many events, like the Goth Weekend, invite creative participation. Consider bringing costumes or accessories that match the event's theme to immerse yourself in the experience.

- **Reusable Items:** Eco-conscious travelers should bring reusable water bottles and tote bags for food and souvenir purchases during festivals.
- **For Boat Trips:**
  - **Warm Layers:** Even on sunny days, the sea breeze can be chilly, so a windproof jacket or warm sweater is a must.
  - **Seasickness Remedies:** If you're prone to seasickness, pack motion sickness tablets, ginger chews, or pressure bands to ensure a comfortable trip.
  - **Waterproof Bags:** Protect your phone, camera, and other valuables from splashes with a small waterproof bag or case.

Packing with specific activities in mind enhances your ability to fully enjoy all that Whitby has to offer.

Staying Connected with Wi-Fi and Mobile Services

While Whitby is a quaint and historic town, staying connected is easy with the right preparation.

- **Wi-Fi Access:**
  - Many hotels, guesthouses, and cafés in Whitby offer free Wi-Fi for guests and customers. Popular spots like **The Magpie Café** or **Botham's of Whitby** are great places to relax while staying connected.
  - Public Wi-Fi is available in areas like Whitby Library and some tourist centers, though coverage may be limited.
- **Mobile Services:**
  - Ensure your mobile phone is set up for roaming if you're visiting from outside the UK. Most UK carriers, including EE, Vodafone, and O2, provide good coverage in Whitby and surrounding areas.
  - Download offline maps and guides in case you encounter areas with weaker signals, especially along hiking trails or rural routes.

- **Power and Charging:**
  - Pack a power bank to keep your devices charged while on the go, particularly during hikes or long boat trips.
  - Visitors from outside the UK should bring a plug adapter compatible with the UK's Type G sockets (three rectangular pins).
- **Local Apps and Guides:**
  - Download local travel apps like **The North York Moors App** or **Visit Whitby** for recommendations on attractions, events, and routes.

With a little preparation, staying connected in Whitby is simple, ensuring you can navigate, share experiences, and access information as needed.

Why Packing and Preparation Matter

Packing thoughtfully for your Whitby trip enhances your experience:

- **For Comfort:** The right clothing and gear ensure you're ready for the weather and activities.
- **For Adventure:** Essentials like maps, waterproof bags, and reusable items support outdoor exploration and events.
- **For Convenience:** Staying connected with Wi-Fi and mobile services allows you to navigate and share your journey seamlessly.

Final Thoughts

A well-packed bag is the key to a hassle-free visit to Whitby. By preparing for its coastal climate, outdoor activities, and connectivity needs, you'll be equipped to enjoy everything this charming town has to offer. Whether hiking the Cleveland Way, attending a festival, or cruising along the harbor, thoughtful preparation ensures your trip is comfortable, memorable, and full of adventure.

Printed in Great Britain
by Amazon